CW00662224

HARDPRESS.NET
HOME OF HARD-TO-FIND BOOKS

Canterbury Tales of the Late Sophia Lee: Consisting of the Two Emilys, and Pembroke, or the Clergyman's Tale ...: the Young Lady's Tale (The Two Emilys) V.2. the Young Lady's Tale (The Two Emilys) (Cont'd) Pembroke, Or, the Clergyman's Tale

by Sophia Lee

Address:
HardPress
8345 NW 66TH ST #2561
MIAMI FL 33166-2626
USA
Email: info@hardpress.net

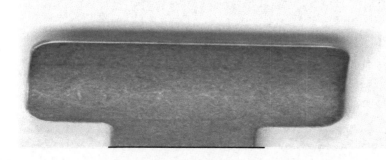

THE
CANTERBURY TALES

OF

THE LATE SOPHIA LEE:

CONSISTING OF

THE TWO EMILYS,

AND

PEMBROKE, OR THE CLERGYMAN'S TALE.

And sure there seem of human kind
Some born to shun the solemn strife,
Some for amusive tasks designed
To soothe the certain ills of life.
                                    SHENSTONE.

THE FIFTH EDITION.

IN TWO VOLUMES.

VOL. I.

LONDON:

PRINTED FOR
LONGMAN, REES, ORME, BROWN, AND GREEN,
PATERNOSTER-ROW.
1826.

LONDON:
Printed by A. & R. Spottiswoode,
New-Street-Square.

ADVERTISEMENT.

THE Canterbury Tales were originally twelve in number; each wholly distinct from the other in character as well as incident, and therefore capable, without injury to the work, of being detached from it: a measure which some circumstances relative to copy-right have rendered expedient.

The " Two Emilys" and " Pembroke" are the only Canterbury Tales that proceeded from the pen of the late Mrs. Sophia iv

Lee, Author of " The Recess:" all the rest were written by her sister Harriet : viz.

MONTFORD,	or	The Englishman's Tale.
ARUNDEL,	. .	The Poet's Tale.
CONSTANCE,	. .	The Frenchman's Tale.
LOTHANE,	. .	The Old Woman's Tale.
CAVENDISH,	. .	The Officer's Tale.
KRUITZNER,	.	The German's Tale.
CLAUDINE,	. .	The Scotsman's Tale.
MARY LAWSON,	.	The Landlady's Tale.
STANHOPE,	. .	The Swiss's Tale.
SEYMOUR,	. .	The Wife's Tale.

February, 1826.

CANTERBURY TALES.

THE

YOUNG LADY'S TALE.

THE TWO EMILYS.

Unaw'd by piety, those, led by will,
Who boldly dare retaliate ill for ill,
Too late, in bitterness of soul shall own,
Judgment and vengeance are with God alone.

SIR EDWARD ARDEN was the chief surviving
branch of an Irish family of that name, lineally
distinguished for birth, and through many gener-
ations very highly allied. He had early married
a *Scots* lady, who ranked kings among her
ancestors; and her prejudices had confirmed his
own, in favour of the rights of the expelled house
of Stuart. Perhaps in this opinion he only indirectly flattered the pride that told him his children might hope much, did a monarch reign to

VOL. I. B

whom they could claim affinity.   Pride has been
justly ranked among the first of human foibles;
but it has one advantage over the rest — it is
generally single in the mind.   A proud man
demands so much of himself, that if his heart is
not the seat of virtue, it must be from his reckoning among his wants, understanding.   Sir Edward
Arden had no other failing than pride: with
bounded means he often contrived to be muni-
ficent; and with many immediate claims on his
feelings, he had yet a stock of sympathy ever
ready for the unfortunate.   Not doubting that he
should meet a counterpart in his sister, Lady
Lettingham, whom he had not seen for many
years, he set out for England in the year 1744,
with two children, whom the preceding summer
had left motherless; resolving to commit these
treasures to the care of his sister, and follow the
fortunes of Charles Stuart.

Lady Lettingham was not without her brother's
failing : though pride in her took not the rich
colouring of virtue.   Distinguished for beauty,
she had early married advantageously, and passed
her whole life within the chilling circle of a court.
The great satisfaction she expressed at finding her

little nephew and niece exquisitely handsome, was soon lost when she understood from their father they were to become her charge, and that he was going to embark in a desperate scheme; the event of which every courtier prognosticated, while the prospect filled them all with horror. The arguments used by Lady Lettingham to detain her brother were so ill calculated to act upon a high and generous spirit, that he only lamented he had exposed himself to hearing them; or sought for his children a guardian so worldly and narrow-minded. The two, inexpressibly dear to him, were yet, however, but children; and he thought that he should certainly return soon enough to prevent their being contaminated greatly, either by their aunt's precepts or example. Finding every effort to change Sir Edward's resolution ineffectual, Lady Lettingham exacted one compliance, which even her brother thought not unwise — to assume the family name of his wife, in taking up arms, that his own might be saved from disgrace, if he failed. Having acceded to this, Sir Edward took a long leave of all dear to him, — for he was among the butchered prisoners, after the battle of Culloden.

Lady Lettingham consoled herself with thinking that the evil ended there.   She wore no mourning, paid her devoirs to the triumphant duke, and ere long got her young nephew recommended to his protection; whose innocent little hand took, from that stained with the blood of his father, a commission.   Her beauty yet gave Lady Lettingham influence; and a nobleman, distinguished for his wit, politeness, and general acceptation, undertook to give the young Sir Edward Arden some of those diabolical worldly precepts which he perpetuated in his letters to his son.

Lady Lettingham having thus, to her own admiration, acquitted herself of the promise to her brother, in taking care of his son, now turned her attention towards his daughter.   Nature had been lavish to the young lady of the dangerous grace of beauty; and her aunt well knew that if the mind could be trained in a certain manner, that might procure the possessor every other advantage.   She had once been near supplanting the Countess of Yarmouth herself; and there would be more kings, as well as more favourites. Anxiously did she practise on a most delicate complexion by delicate cosmetics: anxiously form to every fantastic twist of fashion Miss Arden's rich profusion of auburn hair: now would she sodden, by chicken gloves, to an insipid whiteness, those hands teinted within, by the bounty of nature, with the hues of the rose and the hyacinth; and now check the agile grace of youth, that the drawing-room step, and haughty bend, might early become habit, and a due consideration of the rank of the person spoken to, be always taken into view in the civilities of salutation. All this was, however, duly effected to Lady Lettingham's great satisfaction; and Miss Arden, at the age of fifteen, was as cold-hearted, supercilious, and ignorant, as even her aunt herself. But she had beauty, manner, fashion; and universal admiration sunk on her admirers all her intellectual deficiencies.

Thus to have formed her niece could alone console Lady Lettingham for the misery her nephew brought upon her. He had, most unluckily, his father's failing, pride; therefore knew not how to accept a favour, far less to sue for one. He had another failing, equally incompatible with success in life, — sincerity. To add to his aunt's affliction, he had warm passions, and gave a boundless loose to them. Hardly less lovely in person than his sister, he was surrounded with rich young women, among whom he might have commanded his own fortune, had he not been for ever raving over a dice-box, or masquerading with some kept mistress. Want of money, which makes so many men villains, alone made Sir Edward Arden rational, or good. The generous spirit of his father would then revive in him; and he disdained to be lavish at the expense of other people.

The beauty of Miss Arden soon drew to her aunt's house the amorous, the gay, the dissipated. Lady Lettingham played well, and high: nay, it was thought that she thus half supported her splendid establishment. Those who knew this, chose to purchase the honour of flirting with the beautiful Miss Arden, by a sacrifice of their superfluous cash; while spendthrifts, new to life, imputed those immense losses to love which they should rather have ascribed to ignorance.

The race of life, however, in the higher circles, is soon run: bounded minds, like sickly appetites, are subject to satiety; and it is not so necessary

the object, or the dish, should be superior to the
former, as new.   Miss Arden with astonishment
saw one train of lovers disappear; but another
succeeded, and her astonishment was forgotten.
Lady Lettingham found such a harvest in the attraction of her niece, that she was in no hurry to
dispose of her; and it was not till Miss Arden
found herself a deposed toast, that she ever
guessed her sovereignty was doubted.   Disappointment embittered a mind not without pride,
though without any power to turn that to a generous use.   In this frightful conjuncture she cast
her eyes upon the few admirers who had not yet
deserted, to see if among them she could choose
a husband that might save her vanity — her heart
she had never thought it necessary to consult.
But now her condescension was not less fatal to
her views than her insolence had been.   The man
who understood that the proud fair one meant at
last to marry him, found so many reasons to avoid
the chain, that Miss Arden soon saw herself without a lover.   To be a departed beauty at twenty-
one was beyond all endurance.   She arraigned
her aunt for bringing her out a mere child — the
men for liking the mere children better that had

come out since — and the whole world for not doing justice to her charms. Taste still was her's; and that, happily displayed, might have the effect of novelty. Milliners were worn out; mantua-makers' brains racked; but, however singular — however elegant — the Arden robe, the Arden bonnet, no more became the rage; and Miss Arden was obliged to be overlooked, or to follow the whim of some other miss, who had no advantage over her but that of not having yet satiated the public eye.

Her mother's prayer-book continually reminded Miss Arden she was only twenty-four, when, in the world of beauty and fashion, she saw too clearly that she had become a dead letter. If a young country baronet presumed at an assembly to use his own eyes, and cry out that there was not a woman so handsome as Miss Arden present, the opera-glass of *ton* was instantly levelled — " Ah, Miss Arden! poor Miss Arden! yes, she *has* been handsome: I *remember* her a toast." The stranger stood corrected, and often was ashamed to have given a judgment in which no man of his own age concurred.

Life is not life on terms like these to an acknowledged beauty; and Miss Arden was considering how to change her sphere of action, when the death of Lady Lettingham ascertained her fate. The high style of that lady's establishment made her debts exceed all the property she left behind; and the beautiful Miss Arden suddenly found herself without a lover, a friend, a fortune, or a home.

Sir Edward Arden, on whom, in the helplessness of an unformed mind, his sister threw herself, felt now, even to the extent, the evils of thoughtlessness and self-indulgence. The little fortune he had inherited was already mortgaged — the beauty he eminently possessed already faded — the friends mere kindness might have secured to him, offended by his excesses, or chilled by his neglect, were all withdrawn; and he had now to support and guard a young woman, spoiled by the idolatry of that world by which she was already forgotten; and without one resource in her own mind against its insults or its evils.

It is among the many advantages men possess over women, that they may, if they will, know themselves; and perhaps to that alone may be ascribed their superiority of judgment in all the

great contingencies of life.   Women breathe, as it
were, in an artificial atmosphere; and what hot-
house rose can bear without shrinking even those
genial gales that bring the garden plants to per-
fection ?   Yet, let not the men, therefore, impute
to themselves the power of escaping the universal
charm of flattery; — on the contrary, from its
very novelty, it has, in some instances, such a
wonderful effect, that a well-imagined, or well-
timed compliment from a lady, has, perhaps, ere
now, deposed a king, or made one.

During a country visit to a lady, whom Sir Edward Arden prevailed on to invite his sister while
she mourned for her aunt, it occurred to them all,
that India was a soil rich in wealth, and as yet
unpeopled with beauties; where a young woman,
with merely a tolerable person and reputable introduction seldom failed to make her fortune.
What then might not the highly born, highly bred,
beautiful Miss Arden, promise herself? The Governor, who was soon to depart for that country,
was among those Sir Edward termed his *friends*.
Mr. Selwyn had already brought home an immense fortune from the East, and was now to re-

turn in a high style. Several ladies availed themselves of his patronage and protection, and were to partake his accomodations; but to Miss Arden all gave way: and as Governor Selwyn always presented her his arm, and the first place, she found, even in her humiliating voyage, a consequence, that gratified a mind at once arrogant and weak.

Governor Selwyn was a man not less favoured by fortune than slighted by nature. He was more than *ordinary*, — disgusting. Courage and cunning had, at his outset in life, supplied the place of virtue and fortitude: he therefore had brought back to England rank, wealth, reputation. He lived for some years magnificently; not because he was generous, but luxurious; and he speculated in the Alley, only to multiply those riches which already were more than he ought to have possessed, or knew how to enjoy. The consequence is obvious. A single error undid him. His substantial wealth vanished, but the shadow still remained; and, to impose on his own circle, he even increased that expensive establishment which he had no just means of maintaining. But Governor Selwyn had already lived long enough to know,

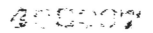

that the only way to get money is not to appear to want it.　He now assured his circle that all things in the East were going to ruin for want of him; and that he could no longer resist the kind urgency, and splendid offers of his friends, to take once more upon him the irksome office, which he thought he had given up for life.　A word was sufficient to make the first tradesmen in London wait on him for orders; and the Governor embarked in all the pomp of Eastern luxury, and surrounded with fair Europeans.

Miss Arden was so naturally beautiful and elegant, and so anxious ever to appear to advantage, that the Governor, having trifled in secret with two or three pretty light coquettes, who laughed at his ugly face and his superannuated gallantry, now resolved to devote himself to this lofty charmer.　He already knew she had no other aim than the other misses——to make her fortune; and that she would value him but as she thought that might be ascertained by his means: yet still he devoted himself to her.　He was certain she was ignorant of the change in his circumstances; and he had cheated his own sex so often, that it appeared a mere amusement to cheat a woman. Miss Arden listened to his gallantry like a well-bred lady who knew exactly how to estimate it. He soon saw, that a rich or handsome rival might step in, and at least puzzle her choice. He therefore became more passionate, more importunate; and that no doubt, on the important subject of fortune, might make her hesitate, he offered to sign a deed, obliging himself to settle the whole of his, on her and her heirs. Miss Arden paused. This was the best offer she had for a length of time had. The Governor might always interfere with her views, if rejected. She could have no more than *all* of any man's fortune. She forgot he was old and ugly, in the remembrance that he was rich : and having allowed him to make a will, as the most secure and simple method of ensuring to her his property, Miss Arden yielded; and the ship's chaplain married her to Governor Selwyn. As each suppressed their motives in the match, love and reason could hardly have given to matrimony more apparent happiness: but, alas! all our enjoyments are uncertain, and this was fleeting, Governor Selwyn died almost immediately on reaching land. His disconsolate relict forgot neither the forms of her situation, nor its rights : but great was her mortification and amazement, when she found herself little richer than at her embarkation. She, however, adroitly availed herself of the example by which she had been duped. The fame of possessing a large fortune is almost equal to the possession of it, if the feelings are not nice. Governor Selwyn was embalmed in great state; and his lovely widow again set sail for England, with all his train of black slaves, Indian canopies, gold services, and magnificent china.

Sir Edward Arden had procured his widowed sister a sumptuous dwelling; and she celebrated the obsequies of her " dear generous Governor" with a grandeur that drew all eyes upon her. — " Ah ! how lovely is Mrs. Selwyn in her weeds !" cried those who could not recollect Miss Arden in her simple mourning for Lady Lettingham. Her doors were besieged, and when etiquette allowed her to open them, lovely, lovely Mrs. Selwyn was again the *ton*. Again her name appeared in the newspaper — again her face was at every print-shop : and all the world bowed at the feet of the rich widow.

But Mrs. Selwyn now knew the world in all-

its ways: and had no time to lose in fixing some
man of rank and fortune yet unversed in them.
In her parties sometimes appeared the young
Duke of Aberdeen.   Through the avarice and
partiality of his father, he had lived till near
eight-and-twenty with little more information or
acceptation than his steward; when a surfeit,
taken at a public feast, carried both his father
and elder brother out of the world, leaving him
sole master of a large fortune, and distinguished
by high rank.   He rolled up to London immediately, with that prodigal splendor incidental to
persons suddenly enriched; and then had good
sense enough to perceive that he wanted every
thing but money to qualify him for superior
society.   The elegant manners of Sir Edward
Arden struck him.   The beauty of his sister
seized on his fancy.   Hardly able from *mauvaise
honte* to reply to her graceful address to him, the
Duke yet adored her for the very ease he wanted:
and Mrs. Selwyn was in possession of the Duke
of Aberdeen's heart, ere the younger coquettes
had woven the light chains by which they meant
to inthral it.   Mrs. Selwyn soon saw her power
in the constant visits of the Duke, and the in-

creasing awkwardness of his address; but the
great advantages of such a match made her readily
overlook the little defects of his mien.

Time, however, showed her, that this unformed Duke had not only strong passions, but
strong sense; and, however easy it might be to
bias the first to her purpose, to act on the last
required most refined address. She therefore
grew more reserved in her conversation, though
more impassioned in her manner. Whenever
marriage was hinted at, she sunk into a tender
reverie; and sometimes on raising her eyes, the
Duke saw those fine eyes flooded with tears. The
indistinct alarm such a conduct caused increased
his affection. He importuned her to confide to
him the care that preyed on her peace, and
blighted the happiness which she allowed him to
hope for. Having wrung from her a promise of
revealing the secret, the lover engaged to come
to her house the next evening, when the door
should be closed on all but himself. The Duke
felt, in this flattering distinction, a full assurance
of success, and past the interval in revolving
every possible cause for the distress of his beautiful
widow, without once dreaming of the real one.

Mrs. Selwyn saw her fortune now at the point of a moment; and omitted no art of the toilette to improve her natural beauty. Her apartment was scented with the rich odours of the East; gauze shades softened every light; a gold muslin robe was girt to her graceful waist with a purple sash, and fell in the luxurious drapery of a Circassian slave: while her heart, throbbing now with hope, and now with fear, gave to her character what it naturally most wanted — sensibility and interest. The Duke of Aberdeen, unused to the world, and to women, felt a strange and exquisite delight, when mysteriously conducted to such a Mahomet-an paradise. No sooner were they alone, than, falling at her feet, he implored her full, her pro-mised confidence. She now entreated his pardon for having given him reason to expect it, but felt herself so utterly unable to avow a circumstance which might rob her for ever of him, that she in vain resolved to be sincere. The anxious lover found fear wrought up to agony : his conjectures over-did the reality, as she meant they should do: in fine, in learning that Mrs. Selwyn had nothing to give him but her heart and her hand, the Duke felt a transport so great, that all the factitious part

of her conduct and character at once disappeared.
A special licence was obtained the next day; and
Sir Edward Arden was summoned to give the
hand of his sister to the Duke of Aberdeen. The
bride had influence enough over her husband to
prevail on him to keep her secret; and his fortune
was too ample to render the payment of her debts
a matter of any consequence.

Elevated almost beyond hope, the Duchess of
Aberdeen had now only one wish to gratify, — it
was to mortify by her magnificence, overbear by
her rank, and humble by her beauty, the whole
circle with whom she had once mixed. But the
Duke had no taste for this kind of gratification;
and to indulge the passion she had inspired,
entreated her to retire to his seat in Scotland,
in terms so strong, that she knew not how to
avoid complying. Her brother took occasion to
point out to her the necessity of showing her
gratitude and affection to the Duke, by other
means than a perpetual self-indulgence. To rid
herself of a Mentor, and weary her husband of his
own plan, the Duchess at length consented to set
out, with a magnificent suite, for her banishment.
That her spleen, however, might have an ob-

ject, when it overpowered her resolutions, the
Duchess carried with her an humble cousin, of the
name of Archer, who was thrown by family de-
rangements on the bounty of Sir Edward, and his
sister Miss Archer had the singular advantage of
engaging the regard of all who knew her ; and for
a very simple reason — neither nature, nor fortune,
permitted her to rival any body. Her features had
every disadvantage of ugliness, but that of being
remarkable; her figure was small, her articulation
imperfect. Accomplishments would have been
unnoticed in Miss Archer, and she had good sense
enough to forbear displaying those which she
indulged herself in acquiring. She had, however,
a mind strong by nature, and improved by literature ; a just and refined taste, and a sweetness of
temper few women can boast. These advantages
are of so little estimation in polished society,
that Miss Archer reached five-and-twenty without
having had it in her power to gratify any passion,
in either accepting, or rejecting, a lover. She had
too the additional vexation of being always a selected person to assist at the nuptials of her young
friends ; and the universal confidante of other
people's love-affairs and griefs, because she had

none of her own to burden them with in return, and showed patient sweetness in hearing, as well as advising. Such a friend might have been the first of blessings to the Duchess of Aberdeen, had she sought by rational means rational happiness : but no sooner was that lady convinced that the Duke's magnificent domains contained not one person worth either charming or fretting, than she sunk into *ennui*. Even her beauty no longer was her care; and when the Duke insinuated any displeasure at her utter neglect of herself, and him, she petulantly asked him, " If he would have her dress for the owls and the daws ;" adding, " that if he meant to see her what she used to be, he must let her mix again with those she was used to mix with." Miss Archer's advice she treated with superlative contempt ; and the Duke of Aberdeen soon painfully felt that his heart was already thrown back on his hands.

In the friendship of Sir Edward Arden, both yet found a solid good, and an equal satisfaction. The generous assistance of the Duke had enabled the Baronet to visit his native country, and pay off a mortgage on his patrimony, without which it would have been added to the estates of the

Bellarney family. The Earl being lately dead, his vast fortunes were vested in his only child and heiress, Lady Emily Fitzallen; who was now first brought out at the Castle, and the beauty of the day. Sir Edward Arden saw her there, and was not himself unseen. Beauty, symmetry, polished manners, and a most winning address, made him a universal favourite among the ladies; and the gentle Lady Emily amply repaid him for the admiration he gave her. The old Countess of Bellarney was unwilling to give up a mortgage so very advantageous, as that of Sir Edward's patrimony. Many conferences ensued, at which Lady Emily was sometimes obliged to be present; at length the Countess, to her infinite surprise, far from keeping Sir Edward's estate, understood that Lady Emily was ready to bestow on him all those she inherited. The old lady's consent was unwillingly wrung from her; and Sir Edward suddenly found himself possessed of a most lovely and tender bride, with half a principality as her fortune. Time had corrected his love of dissipation, and every other foible, which bounded circumstances, and boundless wishes, had produced in him, during the early period of youth :

c 3

and his high spirit, glowing heart, and refined
character, so completely endeared him in a few
months to Lady Bellarney, as well as to her
daughter, that his will became no less a law with
one than the other.

Sir Edward constantly corresponded with the
Duke; and, in the description of his domestic felicity, sharpened the pang of disappointment in his
brother-in-law's heart. Yet in the hope of an heir
the Duke found his affection revive; and as Lady
Emily gave Sir Edward the same prospect, it was
gaily agreed between the husbands, that the lady
who was first enough recovered to travel, should
come to the other. The delicacy of Lady Emily's
habit made her a severe sufferer for some months,
when she became the mother of a sweet little girl.
Great was the delight of Lady Emily; but, alas !
brief. A cold taken by quitting her room too
early, to visit the Countess who was seriously
indisposed, brought on a fever, so delicate a
subject could not struggle through; and the distracted Sir Edward lost at nineteen the idol of
his soul. So acute was his grief, that his health
severely suffered. The scene of such exquisite
felicity became odious to him ; he assisted with the

old Countess at the baptism of his daughter, called her by the beloved name of Emily, and bathing her with tears, committed her, with all her vast fortune (for by the will of Lord Bellarney it was so to descend) to the charge of her grandmother, and resolved to seek, in the society of his sister and the Duke, for the peace which he despaired even with them to find.

And well might he despair; for peace was already wholly banished from the seat of the Duke of Aberdeen. Born to love and hate with vehemence, that nobleman no sooner found that his wife took no pleasure in exciting the first passion, than she exposed herself to become the object of the last. Yet the impassioned heart will have some object, and none was within reach of the Duke but Miss Archer. She had no attraction save mind; yet, in the tyranny of a beauty, that was first brought to light. The Duke soon studied her convenience, soothed her wounded pride, found her necessary to his happiness, and well knew how to make himself so to hers. Exquisitely susceptible of gratitude, Miss Archer perceived not the danger of indulging its emotions, nor how fine that fibre of the human heart is by which the pas-

sions communicate.   Hers were all awakened by the
Duke, who better knew how to calculate his own
influence than she did.   Honour, feeling, every
right principle bade him spare the young woman
who had no other good than the one, which he
might rob her of; but she loved him, she alone
loved him; and, in giving her up, he destined himself to know only a chilling existence.   He ventured, in a moment of loneliness, some dreaded
mark of partiality; and surprised at a novelty like
that of being beloved, a fearful kind of pleasure
caused an exclamation from Miss Archer, but ill
calculated to check a lover: the Duke felt his
power, and soon won her.   The bitterness of her
remorse even in yielding, the excess of her tenderness, the reproaches she lavished on herself, and
the anxiety with which she sought to keep alive in
his heart even the passion she arraigned, all acted
upon a strong character like the Duke's, and
bound him wholly to her.

   Tired of the constraint both were under in the
house with the Duchess, the Duke often importuned Miss Archer to quit it, for a hunting-lodge
he had at a little distance, which by his orders was
already elegantly fitted up for her; but the bound-

less passion she had for him made her rather endure all the humours of his wife, than lose that portion of his society, which she must give up, were she to accept this disgraceful, though safe, home. Yet the situation she soon found herself in showed her removal to be a measure she must ere long yield to.

The pregnancy of his wife caused a public joy, and that of Miss Archer a secret one, to the Duke. He passionately desired a son ; and therefore, as far as possible, indulged the whims of the Duchess, while soothing more tenderly her guilty rival. A delicacy of mind, which Miss Archer still cherished, made her anxiously conceal her situation ; nor had the Duchess any suspicion of it, when one day, the dessert being on the table, the two ladies cast a longing look on a peach of singular beauty and size. Both at one moment reached out a hand to take it ; but the Duchess, as the nearest, succeeded. Miss Archer struggled for a little while with her sense of disappointment, when, after changing colour many times, she fainted away. The exclamation of the Duke, his suddenly starting from his chair, his manner of caressing the guilty insensible, together with the enlargement of her person, on

which the Duchess now fixed her eyes, in one moment unfolded to that weak and furious woman
the whole truth.   The frenzy of her passion could
not be controlled ; she exhausted herself in re-
proaching her husband ; and, seeing her wretched
cousin beginning to revive, reviled her in the most
opprobrious terms.   The only effect of this rage
was to make the Duke throw aside all regard
to decorum : he avowed the guilt she charged him
with, but bade her find in her own violent and
selfish temper his excuse ; and, soothing the unfortunate and silent Miss Archer, admonished his
wife to imitate at least that part of her cousin's
conduct.   The Duchess, exasperated beyond all
speech, threw herself into violent fits ; and the
Duke, having ordered the servants to convey her
to her own apartment, led Miss Archer to hers ;
and leaving at the door several domestics, he
charged them, at their peril, neither to admit the
Duchess beyond that threshold, nor any of the
family attending on her.   He now went to visit
his wife, who refused to see him ; and having given
orders to her women no less carefully to guard her,
he withdrew.

The weak and guilty Miss Archer, who had

against her better judgment sacrificed her virtue, recovered from insensibility only to sink into despair. The Duke, on his return, finding her in its extremity, spared no effort to reconcile her to herself, and to those indignities and sufferings from which he could not save her. He solemnly vowed, that as soon as the Duchess should have given him an heir, he would separate for ever from her; and in the interim her own safety should be assured by her going immediately to the *lodge* already prepared for her reception, whither he likewise meant to retire, till his wife should come to reason. The physician he had sent for now arrived, and finding Miss Archer had strong symptoms of premature labour, ordered her not to be removed. The Duke having repeated his injunctions concerning her being unmolested, mounted his horse, and rode to the *lodge*, to meditate more at leisure.

The Duchess of Aberdeen, having no complaint of the heart, was not long a sufferer. She no sooner understood that the Duke had quitted the house, than, notwithstanding her situation, she flew to Miss Archer's apartment, to thunder in her ears the flaming indignation she was yet bursting with. The servants posted at the door resolutely opposed her entrance; and after threats and solicitations, she was obliged to retreat. The suffering Miss Archer repeatedly sent humble letters, and messages, expressed in the most penitent and moving terms, to her cousin; but these only added fuel to the fire. The Duchess exhausted language to compose her answers, without finding any words bitter enough to express her feelings.

It was at this trying crisis that the melancholy widower, Sir Edward Arden, landed from an Irish bark on the shores of Scotland, and rather chose 'to be his own harbinger, than have notice given of his approach. Confused and astonished at sight of a guest so unexpected, the servants, by their eyes, referred Sir Edward from one to another, when he inquired for the Duke. Wholly occupied with his late loss, and his own sufferings, the Baronet, upon seeing the strange confusion caused by his arrival, was struck with the idea that his sister had ended her days in the same miserable manner with his Emily, when he suddenly heard her voice in no very harmonious key. He flew to her arms, and remained long there (for he fondly loved her), lost in affliction and tears : those which she shed he for some time imputed only to sympathy for his recent calamity ; but observing, at length, that they redoubled when he spoke of the Duke, and that her cheeks burnt with anger, he entreated her to confide her soul's inmost care to a brother who adored her. The haughty imprudent Duchess gave way at once to all the frenzy of her jealousy : she related the past scene with every aggravation which her fancy suggested, while all the faulty part of her own conduct was unmentioned.

Having shown Miss Archer in a light sufficiently odious to exasperate Sir Edward, the Duchess implored him to assert an authority which she had not; and first turning the Duke's servants from the door of Miss Archer, then employ his own to expel her from the mansion, into which she had first brought guilt and misery ; declaring this to be the only satisfaction which his interference could give her. Sir Edward felt even to the utmost the unworthy conduct of the Duke, and the representations of his sister ; but his generous nature revolted at the idea of thus expelling a wretched woman, who might be more unfortunate

than culpable; nor would he promise to be guilty
of inhumanity, however worthless the object.
After pausing, he required of his sister a little
time to prepare his mind and regulate his conduct;
then pressing her hand, assured her, that she
might safely entrust her cause to his care, since he
would either restore all her rights, or revenge her.

.Sir Edward walked out to ruminate on this
singular *éclaircissement*, and form an eligible plan
for quietly removing Miss Archer, as the primary
step to reconciling the married people. By the
account of the Duchess he in fact believed his
cousin to be the sole aggressor, and of course the
single object of punishment. — The bark that
brought him over was yet moored in a little creek;
it was manned by some Irish fishermen, whom an
extraordinary payment would easily persuade to
go to France; and his valet might by the same
means be won to take charge of Miss Archer, and
lodge her in a convent where his interest, and
liberality, he was sure, would confine her. — This
appeared a safe and eligible plan, should the
imprisoned lady adopt it voluntarily. Yet he could
hope to win her compliance only by one method
— the idea that it was the wish of the Duke,

who had chosen this mode of removal, that he might avoid further exasperating his wife, or endangering her own safety.

Sir Edward had received many letters from the Duke, and he passed part of the night in counterfeiting his hand. At length he thought himself sufficiently successful to write a billet to Miss Archer. He informed her, that, learning Sir Edward Arden was arrived, he was doubly unhappy about her safety; he advised her to escape ere his imperious sister should have enraged the Baronet by her story, adding, that, to secure her from pursuit, he had sent a small vessel, with a woman to attend her. She had only to steal in the dusk of the evening alone to the garden gate, nearest the beach, where she would find that woman and a mariner waiting to conduct her to the bark. Early in the morning Sir Edward Arden confided his plan to his valet, who readily undertook to execute it; when, having charged him to fix on some woman capable of assisting Miss Archer, should the pains of child-birth seize her, and who should be provided with every accommodation a person in expectation of them required, Sir Edward thought he had fully acquitted himself of the duties of humanity, as well as of his promise to his sister.

The frail Miss Archer had a little recovered, when the news of Sir Edward's arrival almost caused her to relapse. The quiet that succeeded lulled her into a false security; and his letter, which was delivered to her in great secrecy, as from the Duke, seemed a comfort sent her by heaven itself. Without once reflecting on the improbability of the Duke's being awed by the arrival of any one into a mysterious underhand proceeding in his own house, Miss Archer waited impatiently for the appointed hour which was to enfranchise her. When that approached, she desired to pass the servants directed to protect, but who had no authority to imprison her; and stealing through the garden, blessed the moment that put her into the power of those whom she found waiting for her. Sir Edward's valet sent him, at the moment the vessel set sail, the glad news of her having voluntarily, and unobserved, embarked. Sir Edward hastened to inform his sister, without speaking of his arrangements, that she had for ever got rid of her troublesome and formidable rival; when the Duchess, subject to extremes, in a transport of gratified revenge fell into labour, and soon gave birth to a fine boy. This event caused a jubilee in the family : the servants vied who should fly first with the news to the Duke, and Miss Archer was in a single hour forgotten.

During the time he had been obliged to spend in solitude, the Duke had reviewed his past conduct; and, even giving all the weight self-love could to the faults of his wife, he had not been able to acquit his own heart. Miss Archer, however tender her claim to compassion, escaped not her share of blame; and not all his understanding could reconcile interests so opposite, or fix on the point of morality, without sacrificing feeling or honour. He had half resolved to abide by his duty, even though he should for ever renounce Miss Archer, when he was informed of Sir Edward's unforeseen and unwished arrival. In the expectation of a challenge, the Duke relinquished all idea of conceding to his wife; and he found, with astonishment, a whole day passed away, without either brother or sister taking any step in which he was a party. This moderation on the part of Sir Edward, the Duke considered as a fa-

vourable omen; when the amazing news, that Miss
Archer had, by her own choice, withdrawn from
his house, and that the Duchess had brought him
an heir, at one moment reached him.   Convinced
that no force could have been used to Miss Archer,
the Duke imputed her removal only to the good
offices of his brother-in-law,' and called for his
horses, impatient to return home. He was, however, met on the way by Sir Edward, whose face
conveyed to the Duke the tenor of the conversation he wished to hold with him. The servants
retiring, Sir Edward haughtily inquired if he was
returning to atone for the wrongs he had done his
helpless wife. The Duke replied, that he considered the question as a challenge, and demanded his pistol. A word must have made them
friends or foes, and to be the latter was thus their
choice. They passed behind a thicket, and dis-
mounting, the Duke stood the fire of Sir Edward;
then gallantly and firmly returned it. Sir Edward's second ball grazed the shoulder of his
antagonist, who, throwing down the remaining
pistol undischarged, cried out, " You have had
your revenge, Sir Edward; and now, without attaching to myself an odious imputation, I may

own I have erred. Forget that error, and let this embrace renew a friendship, that will, I hope, end only with our lives."

Who could resist so generous an enemy?— Sir Edward embraced the Duke, and felt that his sister must have been wrong, though he knew not how. The servants saw them return unhurt, and arm in arm, with a joy they dared not express, and knew not how to dissemble. Sir Edward desired permission to hasten on, and prepare his sister to receive her husband. With infinite tenderness he imparted to her the whole proceeding; assuring her, that if he had the least knowledge of the human heart, gentleness and affection would for ever bind the Duke. If, therefore, she prized her present or future happiness, she would never recal the idea of Miss Archer for one moment to his mind; but by cherishing his tenderness towards herself and child, strive to make that unfortunate woman forgotten.

The Duchess's present situation had subdued her turbulent passions. She thanked her brother affectionately for his counsel, which she promised to follow. Sir Edward now conducted the Duke to her bed-side, and left them together. The

Duchess never looked more lovely than in the
maternal character, and she was quite the mother.
She held out one hand to her husband, and, with the
other, pointed to the fine babe who lay sleeping beside her. A thousand tender and hitherto unknown
sensations rushed through the frame of the Duke.
He sunk on his knees, and now kissing the hand
of his wife, and now the infant, entreated her to
pardon, and rely on him. Tears were the general
conciliators; and, from this time, the Duke and
Duchess of Aberdeen began mutually to concede,
and live well together. Sir Edward enjoyed the
happiness he had made, and gave his own name to
the young Marquis of Lenox, whose baptism was
celebrated with princely magnificence.

The Duke, from time to time, vainly hoped Sir
Edward would impart to him the retreat of Miss
Archer; but, as her name never escaped his
brother's lips, the Duke determined to rely on his
honour, in having properly provided for her, and
to show his sense of the generosity by silence.
Sir Edward himself was not so easy. The time
that had elapsed ought to have brought back his
valet, yet he came not. He wrote to France —
Miss Archer had not been heard of: — he then

had enquiries made for the fishermen, and their bark, at Bellarney; but they had never returned; and Sir Edward, after many investigations, was obliged to conclude that the unfortunate woman, whose destiny he had ventured to decide, had found in the ocean a premature grave, together with the infant she was on the point of bringing into the world. Melancholy was so much the habit of his life since the death of Lady Emily, that even this gloomy impression added little to it. Time — the good consequences resulting from the sending away Miss Archer — and other contingencies, at length wore from Sir Edward's mind the painful recollection of her sad and untimely fate.

The limited understanding, and advanced age of Lady Bellarney, together with the infancy of his daughter, made Ireland a cheerless and unpleasant residence to Sir Edward. Both the Duke and his sister delighted in his society; and, save those periodical visits to his Emily, which the tender remembrance of her mother exacted from Sir Edward, he passed many years with relatives so beloved. The little Marquis, growing thus under the eye of his uncle, became his dearest care, and almost the sole

object of his affection.   Delighting to instruct the
lovely boy, Sir Edward made the office of preceptor
almost a sinecure to the gentleman entrusted with it.
Nor was his fondness for his nephew to be termed
partiality.   The Marquis of Lenox joined to a
beauty not less striking than his mother's, manly
grace and mental energy, together with insinuating
address and polished manners.

When Sir Edward left this beloved youth, to
visit the blossom blowing in the wilds of Ireland,
how would his soul melt over the gentle image
of his heart's dear Emily.   Miss Arden already
blended enchanting softness of manners with a
frankness in which her father delighted.   It was
much, though vainly, his wish to educate her in
England, and insensibly lead her heart towards
that of the youth whom he fondly thought he
could at any time lead towards her.   This project by degrees took possession of his whole soul.
He suggested it to the Duke and Duchess, who,
seeing in Miss Arden the sole heiress of two
great families, and an immense property, adopted
the idea with all the facility her father could
desire.   The gentle Emily heard so much of her
accomplished, her beautiful cousin, that all the

vague indistinct attachment her early feelings
allowed, followed the bent of her father's; who,
triumphing in the soft blush which the name of
the Marquis now always called into her cheek,
saw, in the ardour of his soul, its darling project
already realised. Sir Edward had not, however,
calculated all the prejudices he might have to
contend with. The Marquis of Lenox, born to
a title of the first rank, an immense estate, great
natural, and, in time, acquired advantages, felt a
haughty independence of mind which neither of
his parents ventured to overrule. He had from
his birth been such a general concern — so inexpressibly dear — that to find himself irremedi-
ably bestowed in the most important of all points
shocked and offended him. That constraint, at
which all young minds revolt, appeared to him a
peculiar hardship, and the little rustic in the
wilds of Ireland a most unsuitable wife for a
nobleman, who, as all the family flatterers declared, might choose, and reject, in any house in
England. His mistaken parents, and fond uncle,
increased his disgust, by reckoning on his pre-
possession; and the health of his little wife was
at length a matter of ridicule to himself and his

young companions. As time ripened his judgment, he recollected that this *little wife*, this
early betrothed, was the daughter of Sir Edward
— that uncle, whose indulgence for him knew no
bounds : — still she was a mere rustic, and a
bride imposed on him. Therefore, to avoid seeing
her, and break a tie, involuntary on his part,
became the sole object of all his plans. Miss
Arden and her cousin were eighteen, and Sir
Edward had made many unsuccessful attempts to
carry him over to Ireland. Now he was sick —
now engaged in a shooting party — now obliged
to appear at court — or, when all other excuses
failed, the Marquis had but to assert his influence
over his weak mother, and she would declare
that her death must be the certain consequence
of his leaving her a single month. A little piqued
at delays which he could no longer misunderstand, Sir Edward departed, at length, without
even inviting his nephew; having been much
pressed to visit Ireland by an anxious alarming
letter from his daughter. On arriving there, he
found, a very common effect of dotage, that a
young woman, reared and educated by the bounty
of Lady Bellarney, and who was for many years

the humble companion of Miss Arden, had, through the indulgence of her aged benefactress, assumed to herself an authority and consequence very mortifying to a creature too gentle to check the insolence she suffered by. Emily Fitzallen, for this upstart was Lady Bellarney's goddaughter, had, by perpetual attention, and mean adulation, almost shut out the young heiress from the confidence and society of her grandmother, who had been gradually persuaded by this cringing assiduous friend, that Miss Arden was wanting in both affection and duty.

The concessions which Sir Edward recommended to his daughter, as the most likely way to recover her influence, and displace the encroaching favourite, were, by her means, treated as mean and servile in Emily, whose life would have been without hope or happiness, had she not imbibed the fond impression her father had so often sought to give her, of the young Marquis. She languished to visit England, that she might improve the partiality she had been taught to believe mutual, and judge how true the representation made of his charms and graces had been. She had asked for his picture, and her father brought it to her: but, though the Marquis never demanded hers in return, Emily was too new to life to be struck with the slight, and contemplated *his* every hour with increasing partiality. Finding how little the old countess valued her society, Miss Arden, at intervals, desired leave of absence to visit her mother's more distant relations; but, even for that indulgence, was obliged to humble herself to her former companion.

Miss Emily Fitzallen was not less distinguished for either natural or acquired advantages than the heiress. Though of too obscure a birth to bear to have her origin investigated, she had a graceful and majestic mien, that often made her mistaken for the Lady of Bellarney. Miss Arden had blue eyes, long fair hair, and a look of the most exquisite feminine delicacy: the eyes of Emily Fitzallen were dark, penetrating, and impressive. Her complexion was of the white rose teint; and she vainly strove to blend with haughtiness of countenance that sweetness which was foreign to her nature, though the genuine expression of her fair companion's.

In a little excursion which Miss Arden was permitted to make, with a neighbouring young lady

newly married, it was proposed that the party
should cross the channel in a pleasure-bark on the
estate, and surprise the sister of this lady by an
unexpected visit. Miss Arden alone interfered
with the execution of this plan : yet who so much
desired it? To breathe the same air with this
irresistible cousin — to have but a chance of seeing him unknown — romantic thought! what girl
of eighteen could reject it? Despairing to obtain
Lady Bellarney's permission for the little voyage,
Miss Arden suggested, that, if she assumed another
name it might never be known she had been of
the party. The idea charmed them all — they
vowed profound secrecy, and the anxious Miss
Arden thus came at once upon her fate. .

This scheme was not however quite so unstudied as it appeared. The two married sisters
had agreed to convene a large party of the young,
the gay, and the agreeable; and those who headed
it well knew the betrothed lovers must necessarily
meet, although the Marquis would not be aware
of his own predicament.

In a large party an individual excites little
attention; but the consummate, though simple,
grace of Miss Arden attracted universal observ-

ation. Her young heart throbbed without ceasing
when she found that she was really going to see at
last this cousin, on whose perfections she had been
taught to dwell; while he, unapprised of the
anxious expectation he excited, loitered by the
way; and the masquerade, which was to be the
last fête, came without the Marquis of Lenox; yet
still he was hourly expected. Never had Emily
found it so difficult to arrange her dress. In this
solitary situation she had little variety, and no
resources; but true beauty never appears more
conspicuous than when thus thrown upon itself.
In the habit of an Italian peasant, her neck and
shoulders half covered with her rich profusion of
fair hair, a mandoline in her hand, and the light
air of a Grace in every step, Miss Arden appeared
more captivating than if arrayed in all her mother's
jewels. A buzz in the pavillion when she entered,
informed her that a knot she now first saw were
the persons newly arrived, and a glance, that one
of the dominos must be the Marquis. Her heart
instantaneously made its election, and "Oh if
that should not be my cousin!" sighed Miss
Arden. Yet with the anxiety of the moment no
mortification was blended. Accustomed to con-

sider the husband elected for her as the being on
earth whom she would have chosen for herself,
Emily knew not the revolting spirit man often
thinks virtue.   Surrounded by a crowd of unin-
teresting admirers, Miss Arden studied in vain
how to attract the notice of the elegant stranger
her heart had inclined to ; and whom she learnt,
by the flying whisper of her friend, to be the right
person.   That very notoriety she shunned proved
in reality the allurement by which the Marquis
was drawn.   " Who is that graceful Italian peasant,
with the redundant locks of fine fair hair ?" was
his inquiry often repeated, and always in vain.
" The fair stranger," was the general reply. *Fair*,
indeed, thought he, if her face answers to that
light and delicate figure.   He hovered near
awhile.   Emily forgot the crowd that surrounded
her.   He spoke, and she heard in the whole
busy circle only the voice of the Marquis.   He
lamented his loss in not seeing her face ; or rather,
he added, he ought to congratulate himself, as
his fate would then have been for ever fixed. The
timid air with which this interesting stranger
answered gallantry so general something surprised
him ; but he imputed her embarrassment to being

unused to these meetings, and still followed, still
flattered her. An irresistible something in the
tone of her voice fascinated him : yet all it uttered
bespoke a mind so sweetly formed — a soul of
such sensibility — that he felt afraid to treat her
as a common character. "She is no masque-
rader," cried he to himself; "now let me address her more respectfully : and, to convince
her that no impertinence is meant, I will show my
own face." That beautiful face, so highly expressive of sense and sweetness, caught the eyes of
Miss Arden, and impressed itself for ever on her
fancy. The fine flush of agitation, hope, and a
full room, heightened every glowing charm. His
gay and pleasant air, the variety of his manner, in
answering such numerous addresses as the freedom
of the place authorised, and the delicate way in
which he interposed between this unknown charmer,
and every light speech made to her, more than
delighted, fixed Miss Arden. "But dare I hope
to gain such a creature?" sighed she : "or even if
I do, dare I think it possible to keep him?"

They were now in an illuminated walk, leading
from the pavilion to the house. The Marquis
had distanced her masqued admirers, and the

saving her from falling, when she accidentally slipt, left him in possession of the softest whitest hand in the world. He addressed her at once with more distinction, and more rationality. The delicacy and justness of her replies enchanted him. This is indeed a creature to share one's life with, thought he; and Miss Arden felt that he more passionately grasped the hand she was not prude enough to draw from him. Love insensibly became the subject of their discourse; he found the little white hand tremble. "Good!" thought our young man, "I would have it do so;"—but before he had sufficiently recollected himself, Miss Arden was again mistress of her mind. "No, my lord," said she, with a gay raillery, in return to some fond avowal of his partiality, "I will never be a receiver of stolen goods; and when I tell you that it has been whispered to me your heart was allotted ere you knew you had one to give, you will not be surprised at my doubts of my own power over you." Emily now drew her hand from him, and was lost in a brilliant crowd. "And who are you," cried the Marquis, pursuing her with his eyes, "who know so well the foolish bargain made for me? I must follow, and render the knowledge

mutual."—In a moment the Marquis was again
at the side of Emily, with whom he again gaily
trifled, till the crowd dispersed.—" Never will
I part with my fair Italian," cried he, grasping
her hand as if he then felt it to be his own for
life, " till she does more justice to my sensibility,
than to suppose I shall ever deign to take a wife
chosen by others; and to my taste, than to conclude a little unpolished rustic, bred in the wilds
of Ireland, and my perpetual ridicule, would be
that wife."—The Marquis ceased to speak; but
how was Miss Arden to reply?—" He hates, he
despises me!" exclaimed she mentally:—" the
Marquis of Lenox, my betrothed husband, the
man whom of all men I alone can love, loathes
the wife imposed on him. And have I been so
deceived? Oh unfortunate Emily! undone by
too much kindness."—Finding the charmer replied not, the Marquis pursued his discourse:—
" You, whoever you are, who know me so well,
need not perhaps be told that I have never seen
this redoubtable, troublesome, uncouth cousin of
mine: need I add, that I never intend so to
mortify my eyes."—" Never, never, shall you,"
sighed to herself the afflicted, yet incensed,
Emily. To him she spoke no more; but attend-

ing to the indiscriminate compliments of the many
who hovered about her, took the first opportunity
to quit the masquerade, and hasten to her own
apartment.

Alone, tearful, mortified, dejected, she threw
aside her mandoline, and hastily tearing off the
gay paraphernalia assumed for conquest, sat down
to quarrel with the lovely face her glass reflected.
" Yes, no doubt I have always been egregiously
flattered : if my father is blinded by my fortune,
and his own partiality, well may the mean, and
the interested, deceive me. I am, I dare say, the
uncouth wild Irish rustic this insolent irresistible
Lenox so frankly calls me; and, but for him, I
had never known it. Yet ah ! why came I hither
in pursuit of affliction? Why invited I the odious
sincerity? Why did I ever see, or, in seeing,
why did I not hate in turn, my capricious, charming cousin — the allotted of my early days? —
Why, in the erroneous choice of my father, did
this weak heart find, or fancy, the most perfect
of human beings? I will not, however, be as
unjust as himself. *He* is certainly all he would
be; and I can only lament the wanting that

superiority over my own sex which he so eminently possesses over his."

Emily now cast her eyes on the elegant dis-
habille her maid had laid ready for the morning.
" What ! to appear again before this cousin —
repeat the same mortifying scene under the scruti-
nising eyes of a large company, many of whom
know both the relationship and the engagement?
No, that I can never, never submit to," sighed
Miss Arden : — " to fly home is yet in my power.
The Marquis is unconscious of the insult he has
offered me; and, in learning it, may hate her
whom he now only scorns. The bark is at my
command, and I may sail for Ireland with the
next tide. There, unnoticed and unknown, let
the little rustic wither. Yes, dear Lenox, this
way I may show a generous regard, which will
one day ensure me thy esteem. Be from this
hour master of thy own resolves ; find the happy
woman who may give thee happiness; nor ever
know that thou hast thus humbled and afflicted a
creature whose dearest hope has long been that
of becoming thy choice."

Emily flew to the apartment of her hostess, to
impart the strange incident of the evening, —

and implore a general secrecy as to her name,
—after which she declared the magnanimous
resolution she had formed of quitting the party.
But this had no sooner the sanction of her
friend's approbation, than a strange kind of regret, a secret ill-humour, made poor Miss Arden
sensible that she had hoped to be entreated
to stay. Alas! she might never more see the
Marquis, and how was she sure that, when he
knew, he would disdain her? But *if* he should,
— that tremendous *if*, ever so conclusive in a delicate and virtuous mind, at once made Emily impatient to be gone. Orders were sent to the
mariners to be ready at sunrise, and Miss Arden
retired to walk about her chamber, — meditate,
wonder, wish,

> —— " resent, regret,
> Conceal, disdain, do all things but forget."

The Marquis of Lenox, in the interim, wholly
unconscious of the malice of his stars, was something surprised, and perplexed, at suddenly miss-
ing the fair Italian ; but naturally imputed her
retiring to heat, fatigue, and the lateness of the

hour. Having inquired her name, and being told
the one she assumed, he threw his head on his
pillow, to dream of the face that to-morrow morning was to present to him in all its beauty.

The sun arose too soon for Miss Arden's wishes;
and the sailors had sent notice that the tide served
at that hour. Eager to be at home, they came for
the trunks, and urged her to hasten to the beach,
which was only two hundred yards below the gate
of the garden. All was dead silence, — the va-
riegated lamps in the walks, lately crowded, were
yet burning: but

"   'Gan to pale their ineffectual fires."

So general had been the fatigue, as well as en-
joyment, that hardly could the servants of the
family open their eyes to unbar the gates for the
fair, the early traveller: those gates that were perhaps for ever to shut her from the object of her
tenderest contemplations: even at the moment of
renouncing him, the sad pleasure of her life —
by the most grievous occurrence become so dear,
at the very point of time that assured her of his
loss. Emily lingered — she sighed — nay, she

wept. — It is true, she insisted to her maid, that her feet were wounded by the pebbles; for not to herself would she own the wound to be in her heart. Seated at length on the deck of the bark, Miss Arden once more wistfully surveyed the hospitable mansion she had, she now began to believe, too hastily quitted. The beams of the rising sun burnished all the windows, but the shutters were universally closed; and Emily saw the idol she sought there only in her heart. "Thank heaven, he knows me not, however," repeated she to herself: yet, though this grateful exclamation recurred every moment, her own soul told her all it knew of comfort was the recollection, that, if he was *very* inquisitive, many of the company could inform him who had excited his curiosity.

The cause of the perpetual delays made by the Marquis, as to visiting Bellarney, was now too clearly explained—too fully understood. "Why, why, my father, would you then deceive me?" sighed Miss Arden: "why studiously bias my heart towards a young man by whom you knew it slighted — scorned? Yet, alas! my father might, like myself, be misled, and the dupe of his own wishes. To complete her mortification, Emily

then discovered that it be would her hard fate to
explain to Sir Edward the insult to which he had
involuntarily exposed her.

Such were, for many a long day, the contemplations of the melancholy heiress of Bellarney, as
she wandered, spiritless, heartless, through that
splendid mansion, which the increasing infirmities
of her grandmother would soon make entirely her
own. The chilling air of Miss Fitzallen, now the
chosen and perpetual companion of the old Countess, and the fretful questions of the invalid, made
Emily often retire from both, as if she felt herself
an intruder. In the solitude of the woods of Bellarney she, however, found nothing repelling,
though the sound of the " wilds of Ireland" yet
rang in her ears, nor could she now ever survey
the fair face her glass reflected without recalling
the idea of the " little unpolished rustic." Yet, by
one means or another, it is certain she passed almost the whole of her time in thinking of a man
who, it was obvious, thought too little of her, either
under her own name, or that which she assumed,
to cross a safe and very short passage in pursuit
of her.

In this Emily was, however, mistaken. The

Marquis had risen, on the morning of her departure, at an earlier hour than usual. He had been more studiously elegant in his undress than his valet had ever known him, and was pacing in a saloon, where a magnificent breakfast was prepared for the whole party, before a creature appeared. Convinced that his Italian could neither hide her luxuriant fair hair, nor lose her graceful mien, he watched the entrance of each lady till the signal was given for breakfast, without his having been able to discover, in the gay group, one whom he could mistake for the charmer. He now ventured a faint inquiry for her. " She sailed for Ireland at break of day," half a dozen ready voices answered. — " Sailed for Ireland !" returned the lover, in a tone of dismay, " while I was stupidly dreaming of her whom I should have attended ! But are you sure she is gone ?" The beaux, as in malice, conducted him to a telescope, which showed him the vessel, though it was hardly visible to the naked eye. Ardour of heart, and impetuosity of temper, characterised our young man ; and it was happy for those allied to him, that he had hitherto been too rational greatly to desire many things, for those he did desire he

never knew how to deny himself : and to prevent
even his wishes · had been from his infancy the
study not only of his parents, but of every human
being around him.

The breakfast, the party, the modes of life,
vanished at once from the mind of the young
nobleman, and he hastened through the garden
to the beach, where a group of fishermen sat
warming themselves in the sun, and leisurely
mending their nets, while their ready boats, now
plucked from, and now thrown towards the shore,
invited them to try the fortune of the day. The
Marquis hastily demanded, if it was possible to
reach the vessel which sailed with the tide of the
morning. " What, with the pretty young lady ?"
cried one of the men, with an arch smile, and
scratching his head. " You saw her, then ?"
returned the eager lover. " Saw her ! ay, to be
sure, we saw her, sure enough ; and so might
you, if you had opened but half an eye ; for she
did look back many's the time and often, and
examine all the windows of the great house. I
warrant she thought somebody would have been
stirring with the lark this morning." — " Ah !
could it be for me she looked ?" thought the

Marquis, while a faint bluah reproved the vanity;
— " No — for then she would have staid — at
least, a few hours. Hoist your sails, however,
my honest fellows, and, if you know the port, let
us follow; here is gold to encourage you."

Already was the boat prepared — already the
Marquis had leaped into it, and his servants were
hastening to embark with his trunks, when a
signal was made which stopped the fishermen. A
man on horseback was in sight, whom the domestics of the Marquis knew to be one of the Duke's.
He waved to them to stay, and presented to the
young Lord letters from his father and uncle,
informing him that the Duchess had had a
paralytic seizure, so alarming, as to leave her
half motionless, and quite without speech. Even
in this state, she by signs continually demanded
her son, who must hasten to her without delay, or
lose, perhaps, the consolation of softening her last
moments.

Never was son more fondly, though to weakness, beloved: — never was mother regarded with
more affectionate devotion. The power of nature
overwhelmed that of passion, and the fair Italian
was no longer remembered. Actuated by the

same impetuosity, however distinct the occasion, the Marquis mounted the horse which had brought the servant, and flew towards home, leaving his suite to follow, for to overtake him was not possible. The Duchess had still some remains of recollection, when her son took her in his arms; but it seemed as if she had struggled to retain her last sigh only to breathe it on his bosom.

For a considerable time the generous affectionate heart of the Marquis mourned a loss which he felt the more sensibly, from seeing how little impression it made on his father; in whom he soon discovered an indifference towards himself never till that period apparent. In truth he had been the bond of union between his parents, and he had long been the only one. The indulgence of the Duke even to him had, however, been merely habit, and diminished daily, as it interfered with that which he thought it right to grant to himself. But neither apathy nor sensuality withdrew from the Marquis the sympathy or partiality of Sir Edward Arden, who had, though he often greatly blamed, always fondly loved his sister, and now joined with her son in deeply lamenting her. The youth whom she had a thousand times recommended to his parental care and attention, became doubly dear as her representative; and the Marquis felt his attachment to this generous uncle so augmented by the tears they shed together, that when the cherished remembrance of the fair Italian presented itself, he rejoiced he had been prevented from following her; since to have been known to visit Ireland, without paying his devoirs to Miss Arden, would have wounded Sir Edward to the soul; nor could the little trip have been concealed had the boat which his father's groom stopt, once put from the shore with him. The Marquis was of an age when the impressions of one week efface those of the last; and he found it a much easier task to give up all thoughts of the fair stranger, than to encounter the formidable heiress to whom he had been so long affianced.

To avoid sealing by word or deed the family compact, till increase of years, or other circumstances, should make him master of his own resolutions, was now the object with the Marquis: and this he thought might best be effected by making the grand tour. He therefore daily found

it advisable to discover deficiencies in himself, not
obvious to any other person; and declared nothing
but a more general knowledge of men and manners could qualify him to fill the rank to which he
was born.   The Duke had been painfully sensible,
in his own person, through life, of the disadvantage
of a contracted mode of education ; and nothing
but the ill-judged fondness of the Duchess had
kept her son so long in his own country.   Since
her death, the Duke had likewise made another
discovery ; — that his son was grown a man, while
he found himself in some respects yet a boy ; while
both the Marquis, and his rational, correct uncle,
were terrible drawbacks on the use of that liberty
he now began again to enjoy to licentiousness.
The choice of the Marquis to travel being applauded by his father, Sir Edward found his opposition would be vain.   Yet mortal was the chagrin
he felt at seeing this darling nephew, with a heart
glowing and unfixed, formed by nature to charm,
and disposed to be charmed, ready to plunge into
the world, where he might so soon be lost, before
his Emily had been allowed any chance of attaching
him to whom she was betrothed.   Perfectly aware
of all the seductions to which an ingenuous open

nature exposes a young man, Sir Edward could
not, to the one in question, insist on what, by
implying weakness of character, often mortally of-
fends self-love.   Nor did Sir Edward Arden fail to
appreciate duly the advantages of his daughter,
although he forbore to represent them.   He well
knew that the Marquis, seeing him live within the
narrow bounds of a scanty patrimony, could form
no judgment of the establishment his daughter's
birth demanded, and to which she was by her
fortune accustomed; yet how, in the calculation of
her rights and her merits, could a proud spirit
bring forward advantages merely accidental,
though often decisive in their effects in the grand
computation of human happiness.   On mature reflection, the fluctuating father gave up the project
of bringing the young people together, and resolved to accompany the Marquis in his tour.
The enthusiastic joy of the young man, when
informed of his uncle's intention, well rewarded
that uncle.

Due preparations having been made, the Marquis, and Sir Edward, were ready to set out for
the Continent, when a courier from Ireland stopped the latter.   Miss Arden conjured her father

to hasten over, as Lady Bellarney was pronounced
beyond all hope, and she had reason to fear that
she not only should be unprotected, in case of her
death; but perhaps insulted by the overbearing
Miss Fitzallen; who now assumed rights, which
the loss of her patroness would either wholly
assure to her, or rob her of. Sir Edward requested the Marquis to delay the tour, till he
could fulfil a duty so important; and having vainly
waited to hear his nephew offer to accompany him,
suppressed as much as possible the bitter chagrin
so mortifying a coldness could not but occasion;
leaving him in London, he therefore hastened to
Bellarney, attended only by his valet, and a groom,
  It was not without reason that Miss Arden
dreaded being in the power of Lady Bellarney's
upstart favourite; by whose means she had long
been excluded from the fortune, as well as favour,
of the Countess. Emily Fitzallen had infinite
address; she had in childhood obtained an ascend-
ancy over a weak mind, which was afterwards
subdued by infirmity and age to imbecility, and
by fondness to dotage. The patrimony of Miss
Arden was, in right of her mother, secure and
immense: but the old lady had great fortunes

which she could bestow by will, together with the mansion of Bellarney, — a family honour it ought not to have been in her power to alienate: this, and all in the Countess's own gift, she had often declared she would bequeath to her *dear girl*, her *tender nurse*, her *young friend*, her *god-daughter*, and *namesake*, Emily Fitzallen. It is true there were some among her neighbours, who would insinuate that this young person had a claim beyond those alleged; — that the old lady had been a *gay widow*, and this girl christened after her, *resembled her very much.* It is certain the Countess never would allow the origin of her *protégée* to be inquired into; and the haughty Miss Fitzallen latterly always threw at a distance those who presumed to treat her with less distinction than the heiress.

How uncertain are ever the resolutions of a weak mind, and tenacious temper! Lady Bellarney had indeed made a will wholly in Miss Fitzallen's favour, and was in so infirm a state as to render her existence very precarious; when, in a luckless hour, this favourite, against the inclination of her benefactress, joined a party going to some races, who had only invited her from

knowing the consequence to which she would
shortly have a right. The peevishness of age,
increased by loneliness, aggravated this little selfish indulgence into a heinous fault. The old
Countess no sooner found herself alone than she
began to bewail the loss of her own dear Emily,
her darling daughter, long laid in the grave. The
poor orphan she had left, then came across her
mind ; but Miss Arden was cold, inattentive — no
matter ! she was better than nobody : and, to her
great surprise, Emily was summoned to keep her
grandmother company. Long the visitor of a
moment only, to pay her duty, and superseded in
every right of affection, Miss Arden had felt, and
consequently appeared, a cipher. It was otherwise now. She encountered no insolent com-
petitor, and soon saw how she could conduce
alike to the personal ease, and mental amusement
of Lady Bellarney. Astonished to find such
tenderness, skill, and readiness, in a young creature whom she had been taught to think wholly
occupied with herself, the old Countess relaxed at
once. During the evening, she confessed to her
grand-daughter her unlimited bounty to Miss
Fitzallen ; and, finally, showed her a copy of the

will. Miss Arden returned it respectfully, and only observed, that Lady Bellarney could never give her favourite any thing so precious as her affection; nor could she live on terms with herself, if she had lost the distinction by any voluntary failure in duty, gratitude, or tenderness. This mild and sweet reproof had full weight with the capricious Countess; and when Emily knelt, as she nightly did, for her blessing, the invalid, throwing her arms round her, hastily committed to the flames the unjust will, made in a moment of mistaken fondness: vowing, that if she lived to the morning, she would dictate one in favour of her grand-daughter; but if she did not, all would by law devolve to her. This important change in her resolution kept Lady Bellarney awake almost the whole night; and finding herself, of course, weaker and worse, her lawyer was sent for. He, in a summary, but regular manner, ascertained to Miss Arden all the possessions of her grandmother; who, with an almost equal injustice, left unnamed, and unprovided for, the young woman whom she had raised so far above her condition; and who had, from childhood, been subjected to her whims.

Till this unlucky hour, Emily Fitzallen had, indeed, sacrificed every pleasure of youth, and principle of honour, to soothing and working on the weak woman, who had repeatedly assured her of an ample fortune. Miss Arden knew it rested with herself to secure the discarded favourite a competence; but vainly tried to have it done in the properest manner, — as the act of the obliged. — So inflexible are the resentments of age, so fluctuating the determinations of dotage.

The whole family loved Sir Edward's daughter too well, to notice to Miss Fitzallen, when she returned, what had been done in her absence; while, to the astonishment of Emily, her grandmother once more yielded to habitual subjection; and in the servile solicitude, and fulsome flattery of her favourite, forgot her sudden sense of affinity, feeling, and regard to herself. It was impossible to guess what might be the *last* will of a woman, who hardly seemed to have any; and when Lady Bellarney expired, poor Emily Arden knew not, but she might be an intruder in the mansion of her fathers.

Miss Fitzallen, who was ignorant of any will, but that in her own favour, immediately assumed to herself the necessary powers of directing; and lamented with all the dignity of the heiress of Bellarney. Her mourning was made exactly similar to Miss Arden's, and as for a mother. With civil inquiries for that young lady's health, she requested to know when Sir Edward would arrive, to attend the opening of the will, and the funeral, *if he chose it;* as well as to remove his daughter from *her* house. In the mean while, she had given orders to the servants, to show every *proper attention* to Miss Arden. Hearing that Sir Edward was hourly expected, she convened not the family circle, exulting in the thought, that by having the will read in his presence, she should effectually mortify a high-spirited man, whose keen eye had often rebuked hers.

To be the object of impertinent politeness, from one born in a manner to wait on her, was a great trial of Miss Arden's temper. Yet, as it was possible she might have the power of retribution too amply in her own hands, Emily deigned not to appear offended. On the day appointed for the reading of the will, the two ladies accidentally met in a narrow gallery; and Miss Fitzallen taking Sir Edward's daughter by the hand, assured her, that she took her *behaviour very kindly;* then with a haughty conscious air added, that she should *find her account in it;* for though the library, with every thing else, was willed to *her, that* should be her *present* to Miss Arden.

At this extraordinary juncture Sir Edward arrived; hardly knowing whether he should take the horses from his carriage, or deign to set foot in a house that he could doubt to be his daughter's. Miss Arden sent, however, to entreat that he would show her grandmother the last respect of following her to the grave. It was the grave of his angelic wife, and Sir Edward yielded. But Miss Arden had greater difficulty to prevail upon him to attend the reading of the will. The high and peremptory air with which Miss Fitzallen had announced herself to be sole executrix, and heiress, of the old Countess, left no doubt among the remote relations of her being indeed so; and though Sir Edward thought it possible a will was extant in favour of his daughter, he thought it merely possible: so bad was his opinion of the artful Miss Fitzallen. The relations and friends of the family who had attended the funeral were invited to the reading of the will; and the self-

named heiress, overwhelmed with modesty, gratitude, and tears, swept her long mourning robes
through the whole train of sycophants, to an upper
seat in the room. — Miss Arden, always distinguished by simplicity, and sweetness, took the
place she had been used to fill in her grandmother's lifetime: and Sir Edward, not deigning
to mingle with the set, leaned on his daughter's
chair, as ready to lead her out, the very moment
any word that offended his ears reached them.

What was the confusion of the mean train who
had bowed to Miss Fitzallen, when they heard
Emily Arden pronounced, both by nature and
choice, sole heiress, and executrix of Emily,
Countess of Bellarney. Miss Fitzallen remained
for a few moments speechless — convulsed — in a
manner distorted. She then outrageously discre-
dited the will; called it a forgery — a base fabrication of Sir Edward Arden, who had ever, she
said, hated and insulted her. But the reign of
arrogance ends with the means. She found hers
was already over. No eye now paid her homage
— no ear now heard a word she uttered. All
parties united to overwhelm Miss Arden with
gratulations, which, knowing their true cause, she

despised; and feeling even for the insolent by
whom she had suffered, she alone spoke to Miss
Fitzallen. The latter, in bitter agitation, entreated to be suffered to look at the will. Her request
being granted, she saw, with mortal chagrin, that
it was made on the very day when she incautiously
left the Dowager alone. "What makes this
young woman so troublesome?" was the chilling
exclamation of those persons who had an hour ago
thought her born to grace her fortune. Again
agitated beyond utterance, Miss Fitzallen sunk
into a seat to which Sir Edward's generous
daughter kindly advanced. " Recollect, my dear
Emily," said she, mildly, " how patiently I have
borne, during my whole life, my grandmother's
partiality for you; nor thus repine that she has at
her death duly considered an affectionate, unof-
fending child. Let me lighten your affliction, not
add to it. I am not yet by years empowered to
say *how* I will provide for you; but be assured the
proportion of fortune I shall offer, if I live to be
mistress here, will not disgrace your education,
or my own; nor shall you ever have reason to
think yourself forgotten by Lady Bellarney, while
Emily Arden represents her." Dashing with su-

perlative insolence the hand of Miss Arden from her's, the disappointed Miss Fitzallen arose from her seat — the natural majesty of her form dilated by passion to an almost fiendlike grandeur — her large dark eyes flashing with supernatural bright- ness, and all the rage of her heart burning in scarlet teints on her cheeks. " Who could mis- lead you so far, Miss Arden," cried she, when words came to her assistance, " as to make you believe that *I* would ever owe any thing to Sir Edward Arden's daughter ? Since he has taught you how to step between me, and the provision long mine by promise, keep it all — dear to you may one day be the acquisition : — your whole fortune could not buy off my hatred, nor could the empire of the world buy off my revenge." — Rushing through the astonished train of gaping relatives, Miss Fitzallen passed the gates of Bel- larney, nor once recollected, till they were closed upon her, that she had not a spot whereon to lay her head, nor one friend in the world anxious to soothe, serve, or receive her. In a neighbouring cabin, gold procured her a temporary home, till her maid could pack up her clothes, with some jewels, and other valuable presents of the old Countess.

On the mind of Sir Edward, the unmatched insolence of Miss Fitzallen had made such an impression, as doubly endeared to him the daughter he found so unlike her. That amiable young lady, at the age of nineteen, mistress of herself, the magnificent seat of her maternal ancestors, and immense wealth, thought so generously, and acted so wisely, that Sir Edward groaned under the secret sense of her cousin's injustice — that cousin whom she seemed born to make happy! New hopes and plans again took possession of his mind. No duty now bound Miss Arden to move in the narrow circle of her maternal connexions; and her father thought it advisable to carry her to England, with a suite and establishment proper for her birth and fortune. Resolving to present her at Court himself, he fondly hoped the Marquis could not behold his Emily without blushing at his own coldness and injustice; and, being led by the lovers she must necessarily attract, to assert his prior claims, and endeavour to win her heart. As it was not possible at once to arrange all Miss Arden's newly devolved fortunes, Sir Edward was obliged to pass some time in acting the guardian, as well as the parent, and often adverted to the brilliant *entrée* she would make under his auspices, in the gay world. Coldness, silence, dejection, always followed, on the part of Emily. " No — she had not the least taste for the world; and would rather, if her father pleased, pass the time of his absence at Bellarney." The vexed father now sighed to himself, " *Both — both* infatuated alike ! — what can be done with them ?"

- In renewing the leases, and other negotiations with the tenants and dwellers round Bellarney, Sir Edward learned a hundred tales of the selfishness, meanness, and overbearing disposition of Emily Fitzallen, who still remained at the cabin she had at first retired to, languishing in a fit of sickness. To Miss Arden's proposal, of giving her a handsome fortune, Sir Edward refused his concurrence; nor could his daughter dispose of aught considerable without his knowledge, after having made him her guardian, as he ever had been trustee. An annuity just sufficient to save this wretched young woman from want and ig-

nominy, Sir Edward thought as much as she
merited. To this Emily could only add her own
jewels, which were indeed a fortune. With these
she sent a kind letter, assuring her former companion, that nothing but her inability to act for herself could have made her appear deficient in generosity or feeling. The jewels she desired to
redeem, when of age, at the price of a proper provision for Lady Bellarney's favourite friend: and,
if she died in the interim, she entreated Miss
Fitzallen to consider them as her own.

Unaltered in mind, though humbled in condition, Miss Fitzallen returned the bond of annuity, jewels, and letter, with sovereign contempt,
and without a line, into the hands of Sir Edward
Arden, who considered his daughter's generosity
as mere weakness of temper. He soon converted
it into an argument in favour of his own plan of
carrying her to England. From arguments, he
came to injunctions; and finally hinted, that, if
she remained without a male protector in her own
country, she would be carried off by the first
fortune-hunter who had half the courage, or assurance, of Emily Fitzallen. This conclusion
appeared so unfair and humiliating to Miss Arden,

that she burst into tears, and declared her fate very
hard.   Sir Edward would know, in what it appeared so.   " I shall offend — nay, I shall, I fear,
pain you," sighed the gentle Emily, " if I am
candid."   Still Sir Edward insisted on the truth.
—" Pardon me, then, my father," resumed she,
" if, weak of character, lowly of mind, as you think
your daughter, she should have pride and spirit
enough to shun for ever the Marquis of Lenox."
Sir Edward started angrily, and gazed intently.
" Why shun him, Emily ?" was all he could utter.
" He hates me, my dear father — he ridicules, he
despises me." " And who dared tell you this ?"
returned Sir Edward, in a tone that admitted the
truth of what she said, though his eyes struck fire
at the indignity.   " Alas ! I could not doubt,
Sir : — it was from his own lips this mortification
reached me.—Controul your emotion, and learn
the whole story.   I do not suppose, that, had he
known, my cousin would have insulted me : — we
met in masks, nor does the Marquis guess, to this
hour, the wound he gave to my heart ; it has been
my misfortune to be imposed on his : had he thought
himself unfettered, I might have had a chance of
pleasing him.   He is now lost. Under these cir-

cumstances, to *force* myself on his notice — insist
on the poor advantages I should in turn despise
him if he valued me for, could not but for ever
disgust a heart which it would be my pride to
convince, my pleasure to win. The little merit
I possess would be lost were we just now to meet,
under the pomp and splendor of my rights in life,
which he no doubt concludes the family reason
for making him wretched. And could a cold compliance with his engagement fail to make me so?
No—rather would I waste the rest of my life in
this seclusion, bewailing the want of his heart, for
whom," faltered the sweet girl with increasing confusion, "I had wholly, I will confess to my father,
reserved my own." Sir Edward hid her ingenuous
blushes in his arms, and fondly prayed to Heaven
"yet to unite those hearts so equally dear to
him." — "I have not told you," resumed Miss
Arden, in the same timid tone, "that I even now do
not despair, if you will leave me to execute a plan I
have meditated ever since I found myself at liberty
to quit my native country. My wayward cousin is,
I must first inform you, a stranger to my features;
nor knows he that it was Emily Arden he cruelly
humbled in the description of herself. Unless

you betray me, I may yet appear before him in any
character I choose to assume ; and I have a romantic fancy afloat in my brain, that I cannot
execute without your concurrence. Return, my
dear father, to England, alone ; urge, persecute
the Marquis to visit me in Ireland ; and, while he,
of all human beings, detests this troublesome overbearing heiress, might he not, on some obscure
spot of his father's estates, stumble on a simple
rustic, with just such a face as mine, and perhaps
love her with his whole heart ? Dennis, my silver-
headed foster-father, may not unaptly personate my
real one ; and become a protector. Think of the
delight we should both feel, if the poor Marian,
in a plaid jacket, should step before your rich
Emily, covered with diamonds. — If, on the contrary, I make this experiment in vain, let it be a
last one. To Bellarney let me return undiscovered :
nor ever allow the Marquis to know that he has
personally slighted the daughter of a man to whom
he has been long endeared by a parental affection."

Age had not yet so chilled the heart of Sir
Edward but that it caught, in a degree, the glow
of his daughter's. The romance was simple —
was safe ; — if he discharged his groom (for he

could trust his valet) — practicable. — While Emily had been thus sweetly insinuating wishes and views so consonant with his own, Sir Edward had considered the soft and unassuming grace of her figure, the delicate turn of her beauty, and the artless eloquence of her voice. He now fancied her in a straw hat, with her fair locks playing round her face, and now adorned for a birth-night; and he plainly perceived that she might lose, but could not gain, a charm, by splendor or fashion. Her plan every moment grew upon his imagination. He saw his prudent Emily, even in her romance, had guarded both his pride and her own. He well knew that he could not brook the having his daughter, as herself, refused, even by this darling nephew; yet he never contemplated the mortal coldness, and probably eternal alienation, such a procedure might cause, without a feeling almost amounting to horror.

After a long silence, Sir Edward embraced his apprehensive daughter, and told her that this experiment had not only his sanction, but warmest approbation; nor would he omit calling upon the Duke, to aid the malicious persecution meditated

against her lingering lover, the more fully to prepare his heart, by the agitation of dislike, for the
reception of a more pleasing passion.   The transport expressed by Emily brought to light all the
power of her soul, and the more dignified graces
of her mien, till Sir Edward half rejected the
scheme, in the firm persuasion that she could not
fail to charm, as herself: but having won his consent, Emily bound him to his word.

How pleasing, though anxious, was her employment, while preparing all things for her obscure departure, and instructing Dennis and her
nurse in the parts they were to act.   When the
Scottish cot should be ready, Sir Edward undertook to inform his daughter; who could then
embark from her own estate.

Nor was Sir Edward without his share of delightful hopes and recollections.   To know the
fate of the two beings most dear to him on earth,
so near a crisis that promised to be happy, gave
his heart those sweet pulsations, which have all
the charm and softness of passion, without its
danger.

And now what became of the Marquis? Why,
he devoutly wished the old Countess " an earthly

immortality." But, finding her soul had made
its escape without his permission, he heartily
prayed he could make his, before his uncle returned to London: for that he would bring with
him this odious Irish heiress was, he thought, too
certain. At the moment Sir Edward's carriage
drove to his father's door, he was coming out of
it: and, what a relief was visible in his features,
when he saw it contained not a female! How
cordial were now their greetings! The Duke,
however, not having the least objection to Miss
Arden's company, inquired why her father had
not, at last, brought her. Sir Edward very
naturally answered, that he had fully meant to do
so, had not some of Miss Arden's romantic
female friends in the interim insinuated to her,
that it would be a high indecorum in her to seek
the Marquis of Lenox; and, from the moment
that whim had taken root in her mind, it was impossible to remove it. Fixed as every thing had
long been for the tour abroad, he added, that he
imagined it would have been irksome to his nephew
had he then proposed the visit to Ireland. A
female, of advanced years, and due consideration,
had therefore been found to give propriety to

Miss Arden's remaining at her own seat, till the tour, which they must now necessarily shorten, should be made; when he hoped the Marquis would be as ready as himself to attend upon his bride elect.

The Marquis, finding the evil day of insipid courtship once again deferred, was no longer in such haste to commence his tour; and heard that law affairs must detain his uncle for some time in town with great satisfaction. This conduct made Sir Edward enjoy, almost to malice, the meditated attack on him, which he meant should shortly come from his father.

In hours of loneliness, Sir Edward recounted to the Duke his daughter's little history of the slight she had borne, and the final effort she meant to make to engage the affections of the Marquis: but the natural delicacy of his mind led him to call the plan his own, and one to which she had with some difficulty consented:—if this failed, he added, "Emily should no longer sacrifice her claims in society to an ungrateful relation who despised her." The Duke was a matter-of-fact man, and easily followed the idea presented to him; nor failed to lecture his son on the disrespect

shown to Miss Arden; which was not only calculated to rob him of all hopes of her heart, but to
induce her to carry into another family the immense fortune she inherited ; while that which he
was born one day to call his own was already in-
sufficient for two men, neither of whom was old
enough to give up his tastes, or young enough to
be controlled in them. It is true that the love,
respect, and confidence which the Marquis once
had for his father had declined from the day of
his mother's death ; but he had not yet learned to
act in opposition to his will. Indeed, till this moment, he had not felt it. The important cause
was argued, and re-argued ; and Sir Edward, by
turns, appealed to, as the judge. He had always
the address to avoid so odious an office; yet his
nephew thought he could perceive that it would be
easier to work on his mind, than on the cold,
worldly, selfish one of his father. How grievous
was it to feel that he had such a father, and to
recollect that his mother brought no fortune into
he family, nor could he claim a guinea during
ne life of the Duke !

The arrangements in Scotland being now made
for the establishing of Emily there, and the feel-

ings of the Marquis wrought up to a high pitch, the two fathers thought proper to find out that his signature, ere he went abroad, would be necessary to some family deeds, which must be executed in Scotland. The recollection of the vicinity of the castle to Port Patrick made the Marquis very unwilling to go, lest his father should drag him to the feet of Miss Arden; yet he ventured not to hint the fear, as that might lead to the determination.

Sir Edward having no need of an English groom on the continent, easily parted with the one who had attended him in Ireland : nor was there a single domestic in the suite of the family party who had ever seen Miss Arden. Arrived within a bow-shot of the cot where she had taken up her abode, whole days passed away without Sir Edward's daring to set foot in it, or even to see his daughter, lest suspicion should follow. He could not persuade himself that it was possible she should conceal her birth, of which her deportment was so expressive ; or avoid, whenever she met the Marquis, the deep confusion that implies design. On full deliberation, Sir Edward resolved to break in upon her by accident ; and in taking a

morning's ride with his nephew and the Duke, affecting to be seized with a vertigo, he almost fell
from his horse. The Marquis and grooms lifted
him off, and assistance was hastily demanded from
the adjacent cot, whence hastened the silver-
headed Dennis; soon outstript by a wood nymph
so exquisitely animated and lovely, that, to the
astonished Marquis, the Graces seemed all embodied in a rustic of Scotland. The disguised
Marian, alarmed with the sudden ailment of Sir
Edward, forgot that the Duke would be a spec-
tator, remembered not the Marquis, even when
their looks met; but sensible only to filial anxiety
and affection, fixed her dark blue eyes on her
father, and gave to herself the first and dearest
charm in humanity, — the having forgotten she
had one. A wicker chair was now brought, and
Sir Edward placed in it; the white hands of Marian
assiduously sprinkled his forehead with cold water,
while drops, more vivifying than art or nature ever
otherwise prepared, fell from her cheek to his.
How sweet was this moment to a father so tender;
to find love itself was lost in the sense of his
imaginary danger. Placed on the humble bed of
Dennis, a valet opened a vein in his arm. Marian,

the ready Marian, prepared and fixed the band-
age; her hand alike administered the cordial;
nor was it till all that could be done was done she
became sensible that she was standing before those
who were to decide her fate; the single object of
their attention. In the eyes of the Duke she discovered that he knew, and, knowing, approved
her. In those of his son she discerned a restrain-
ed, but boundless admiration, — a something that,
passing from his heart to hers, seemed already
to bind them sweetly together, by an unseen but
indissoluble ligament. Sir Edward cast his eyes
from one to the other, and had his full share
in a feeling that made the humble hut of Dennis
appear a paradise to every being it contained.

The Duke had sent for his coach to convey the
invalid home. The Marquis desired to accompany him; and the carriage was no sooner in motion, than each fell into a fit of abstraction, though
in both the same object caused it. The Marquis
at length broke silence; and not having yet had
experience enough to observe that whatever a person first speaks of, after a long meditation, has
generally been its subject, exclaimed, " How
beautiful, how redundant, her fair hair!" once

only. — Sir Edward, not more cautious, added, " and the softest hand in the world — would it were now bathing these burning temples."— " I can fetch her in a moment, uncle," — said the impetuous youth, attempting to open the coach door, and glad of an excuse for returning. " Not for the world, my dear boy — she is young — not ordinary — I would neither trust your father, nor his dissipated servants : — were I to cause her innocence a risk, I should never forgive myself." The Marquis put up his lip in silence : could Sir Edward think so superior a creature could listen to the servants — or be bought by his father ? Sir Edward read this in his face, and saw, in the contempt which the Marquis ventured not to avow, the influence that Marian had already gained in his heart.

The Marquis now again was in no hurry to commence his tour : — he, therefore, less lamented his uncle's illness, though it kept him almost wholly in his apartment — where he often revolved the means of establishing an interest in the heart of this lovely creature : of all whom he had ever seen, she alone reminded him of the fair-haired Grace, who, as an Italian peasant, appeared, as it

were, to enchant, and vanished to bewilder him.——
After many contemplations on the subject, he put
twenty guineas in a purse; and having wandered
doubtfully for some hours round the cot of Dennis,
faintly rapped at the door. — Marian herself opened it: but Sir Edward being no longer present,
to mark, or to divide her attention, so rich a blush
mantled on her fair cheek, as might give the most
modest of men a hope that he had not been unnoticed by her. The Marquis, with a varying
complexion, and timid air, inquired for her mother. —The aged dame rose from her spinning-
wheel, and the silver-headed Dennis from reading
the Bible: each depositing a pair of spectacles in
the case, remained standing to receive the com-
mands of the young Lord. — To behold thus,
in the light of subjection, his charmer, and the
venerable old people, strangely distressed the Marquis. — Had Marian not been there, his rank
would have been less oppressive. —With much
hesitation, he gave them to understand, that Sir
Edward Arden had made him the bearer of his
acknowledgments for their benevolence. He then
put into the mother's hand the purse, and its con-
tents. — " No, no, my Lord," cried the respect-

able Dennis, " that can never be. —Wife, give
his honour back the purse.   Sir Edward sent his
own valet yesterday evening with a present of two
new guineas, fresh from the mint, for our Marian."
The Marquis was struck dumb at what he thought
the meanness of his uncle.   To affront the charmer of his soul, with the paltry gift of two
guineas ! — sent by his valet too ! — He turned
to apologise to Marian, but she had disappeared:
no wonder, when she heard herself and two
guineas spoken of together.   " Well, my good
old friend," said the Marquis, " my uncle might
do the odd mean thing you say, for he has been
delirious, and raves often of your assiduous Marian : — but he is now in his senses, and better
knows how to respect himself and your daughter.
I have no mind to drive him into a frenzy again,
by taking back the little mark of his gratitude."
Having thus said, he laid down the purse, and
ran out of the cot.   Perceiving in a field very near
the plaid dress of Marian, he was at her side in
a moment; — spoke of her generous sympathy —
the illness of his uncle — the wild beauty of the
scenery around, — any thing, every thing, that
might prolong the exquisite pleasure he found in

being one minute the single object of her attention, the engrosser of her thoughts and conversation: yet Marian seldom spoke, and always said
the least she could ; nor did she often raise her
eyes to meet the impassioned glances of the
Marquis. Still a sympathetic charm never to be
defined told him that she was not insensible to his
presence — not willing to bid him farewell.

Neither in the sick chamber of Sir Edward,
nor in the saloon with the Duke, did this Grace
of the woods ever become the subject of discourse ; yet both the fathers were well informed
that the Marquis hovered anxiously, early and
late, near the cot of Dennis, well rewarded if he
obtained but a word, a glance from Marian. —
Sir Edward did not find it convenient to recover
very fast; and never did his nephew think it possible till now that he should dread seeing him
leave his chamber: but to be dragged out of the
kingdom, ere he had time to win on the affections
of her whom he adored, or to bind her to himself by mutual vows, almost distracted him. The
Duke easily perceived his distress and agitation ;
but as the two fathers had agreed that the fear
of losing Emily would best secure the attachment

of the Marquis, by rendering her the perpetual
object of his thoughts, they would not consent to
her avowing herself.

Nothing but the dread of separation, and the
necessity of employing the short time which the
lovers were able to pass together in conversations
respecting the future, could have kept the Marquis in ignorance of the past: for a vague idea
of something mysterious in the situation of Marian,
as well as elevated in her language and manners,
often floated in his mind. — But who, thinking
every look he gives to her he loves may be the
last, can press for details of remote occurrences?

Sir Edward was now ready to depart; the
happiest of fathers to know his Emily had conquered; — that she reigned in the ardent heart
of the young nobleman, who had in secret solemnly
affianced himself to the choice of his parents —
the once dreaded, hated Emily Arden. — Often,
when she saw him at her feet, the glowing exultation of secret triumph so heightened her beauty,
that the delighted lover wondered in vain at its
suddenly acquiring so celestial a charm. — It was
now the precise moment for tearing him from her;
and both fathers again proposing the tour to the

continent, any delay, on the part of the Marquis, would, he easily saw, have led to a discovery of his motive. Every leisure moment he flew to Marian, to lament his untoward fate, and execrate the cold nature of those who thought it possible he should find in the overbearing Irish heiress a creature who could dispute his heart with Marian. — That name, so humble, so rustic, now was music to the ear of Sir Edward's daughter; for under that she had given, and received, vows, which no time, no circumstance, could ever annul.

Sir Edward now suddenly seemed to recollect how proper it would be for him to make his personal acknowledgments to the daughter of Dennis, and chose to have the company of his nephew. The cottagers received the visit with joy and gratitude. Sir Edward very gravely exhorted them to guard so lovely a creature as Marian from the attacks of the Duke, or the humiliation of marrying one of his servants. The Marquis, and his charming mistress, upon hearing this exchanged souls in a glance, not unseen by the watchful Sir Edward. He concluded this exhortation with in-

forming the old people, that whenever they found
a suitable match for their daughter, they might
apprise him, and he would portion and patronize
her.   Ah ! uncle, will you really do this when a
suitable match occurs ? said the intelligent eyes of
the Marquis.

Sir Edward with due gravity allowed the cottagers an annuity of twenty pounds a year, and
departed overwhelmed with blessings : nor was he
himself at liberty to utter one of the many his
heart poured on his Emily. The Marquis no
sooner saw his uncle again in his own apartment,
than he flew back, to reiterate, under a more
flattering and tender form, the same cautions to
Marian.   He made her again promise, vow,
solemnly swear, to live for him, and him alone.
What laws in return did he not impose on himself ! how impossible did it appear to him that he
should ever find a charm in another woman, or
ever breathe to a second object a vow like that he
now blended with his parting kiss, his long farewell. The interesting Marian left on his cheek
the seal of true love, in a tear ; and had the resolution to see him depart in the full conviction

that he spoke only as he thought, and that all
their present pains would eventually complete
their mutual wish.

With the embarkation of the Marquis, Miss
Arden's disguise ended.   She immediately accompanied the Duke of Aberdeen to London,
where a lady was already engaged to sanction her
living in his house.   When presented at court,
the admiration she excited procured her high offers of marriage; though many lovers retreated,
her engagement with the Marquis being universally understood.   Surrounded with her own friends,
and suite of attendants, Miss Arden had no motive for anxiety but the absence of her lover; yet
as that only could prove the truth and the strength
of his attachment, which the most impassioned letters daily confirmed, she had very little cause to
complain of her fate.

And now the Marquis and his uncle were for
the first time in Paris; plunged into that busy
vortex, the world, where the virtues are often at
once ingulfed; and if they ever rise again, it is
in fragments, hardly resembling their first state.
Yet such a guard, on a noble nature, is a true
and tender passion, that the young man found not

the love of pleasure lead to licentiousness, nor
that of distinction to corruption of soul.   The
strongest emotion of vanity he felt, when the object of universal attention, was a faint wish that
the charmer of his heart could know the value of
it, by seeing how many were willing to dispute it
with her.

But what an enviable fate was Sir Edward Arden's ! enabled, unsuspected, to trace to its inmost
recesses the emotions of the heart he best loved;
to see all that was generous and amiable in nature
point to one object, and that one object his own
dear Emily ! Not a letter did the trembling hand
of the Marquis open from her, that the glow of
his cheek, the triumph of his soul, did not announce all he felt to his watchful guardian, who,
thus satisfied that he was relieved from his charge,
gave the young man up to his own pursuits, and
followed those himself that were more adapted to
his period of life.   And if the father thus exulted,
how must the lover, who found in those letters of
his fair rustic, a delicacy, softness, and refinement
which he in vain sought in the rest of her sex ?
for, however cautiously Miss Arden veiled in her
correspondence the high polish of her education,

the feelings of her heart alone gave its sentiments a charm peculiar to herself, while the confiding tenderness they breathed was the dearest of all claims on the faith of him whom she addressed.

Sir Edward, who had ever a turn for study and the fine arts, introduced his nephew, with himself, into the society of all persons eminent in literature and science. The Marquis had a taste for drawing, in which his uncle excelled. As both proposed taking views of the scenes that most should please them, the young nobleman engaged an eminent master, under whose instruction he made a rapid progress; and, ere long, had acquired almost as much knowledge as might perpetuate to his soul the pleasure that otherwise fades on the eye. The season now was at hand when Sir Edward and his nephew proposed following the course of the Loire in their travels. The drawing-master, one day, while they were enlarging on the labours they should embark in, suggested how irksome it ever is to fill up the outline which we delight to throw off the fancy; adding, that he had, among his less fortunate pupils, a youth whom it would be an act of benevolence to employ: he was an orphan, in narrow circumstances, but of very superior talents, who, having no hope of future provision, except by improving and exerting them, would think himself well rewarded in the protection and patronage of two men of taste, if, while humbly assisting them, he might be allowed to employ part of his time in studying the immortal models they must necessarily visit in Florence and Rome. The Marquis, it is true, loved drawing, but he was of an age to love his ease; and this proposal united those advantages. He appointed a time to see the youth, whom, in the interval, he proposed to his uncle as an addition to their little suite. Sir Edward agreed, that if his talents equalled the account of them, to take him would be an act of kindness to themselves, as well as to the boy.

When the drawing-master presented the young man, by the name of Hypolito (for he was the son of an Italian painter who had settled and died in Paris), his extreme youth and pallid looks (for he seemed hardly sixteen, and consumptive) struck Sir Edward, who, with unusual abruptness, urged that objection. The modest lad shrunk back. Tears rushed into his eyes, and the wild air of distress was blended, on his languid countenance, with unmerited humiliation. The Marquis, ever interested by the unfortunate, having cheered Hypolito, sat down with him to draw. The youth took the piece which the Marquis was finishing; and at once proceeding with rapidity, while he touched all parts with elegance, showed at once that he was indeed a treasure to travellers, and a master in his art. Sir Edward was now no less charmed than his nephew. "Nor is drawing his only talent," said his introducer, handing to the youth the flute upon which the Marquis played in a capital manner. Hypolito breathed on it, and the instrument seemed to have the charm of the lute of Orpheus on all but the person who held it; for he, sinking back in a chair, almost fainted. When he revived, the poor lad with blushes accounted for the illness, by confessing that he had not tasted food the whole day. Immediate succour was given him. The Marquis caressed him like a brother. From that hour he cast off the mean garments of poverty — by care, and good living, recovered his looks, and was the constant companion, in all elegant and scientific pursuits, of the Marquis of Lenox. The world had before given him every good but a friend; and that he found in Hypolito. — While Sir Edward saw with delight his nephew filling up his life with so rational a pleasure, many a time did he shiver on the water, or broil on the land, without complaining, when he found their ardent natures bent on perpetuating the scene before them. Sir Edward himself played on the violincello; and seldom did they rest at a town, or village, where they could not add a performer, or two, to the concert, and thus inspirit the evening.

Enchanted with the gay scenery, the romantic pleasures of Italy, the Marquis wanted only his Marian to share the delight; and well could he have been pleased to pass his whole life there. But it had not this charm for Hypolito. From the moment they quitted France, urbanity of manners vanished. In the petty states of Italy, the little souls of the nobles contract into a very narrow circle what they are pleased to call society. Not all the advantages Nature can lavish — not all the acquirements Genius can attain, give acceptation, among that arrogant body, to a man born without a positive rank in life. How, then, can he who supports himself by the exertion of talents hope to be received by those who make it their pride to be without any? Sir Edward and his nephew mixed, as they were entitled to do, in the first circles; but a deep sense of the solitary situation of poor Hypolito, who was in that middle state which made it as impossible he should associate with the domestics, as be countenanced by their lords, often drew towards home the heart, and not unfrequently the feet, of the Marquis; for seldom found he a companion whom he liked so well. — The gratitude and affection of Hypolito induced him to exert every talent and grace, to endear himself to his condescending patron; and, as there is no charm so fascinating to the young mind as that of giving at once distinction and pleasure, the Marquis grew daily more attached to the humble Hypolito. So marked a friendship drew the observation of the Italian nobles, although they wished not to know more of the merit that caused it; yet every day produced a new banter among the set, who, by often rudely staring at the youth, marked a strange doubt of his sex.

Sir Edward began, after passing a year in Italy, to bend his thoughts towards home; and proposed returning to his nephew. The unpleasant recollection of Miss Arden damped the tender one of Marian; and the Marquis found it easier to live without the latter, than to encounter the former; for to marry her came not within his calculation of things. Till the heiress should have disposed of herself, he knew it would be vain to hope he should prevail on either his father or uncle to approve his humble choice; and he resolved to travel to the Antipodes, if Miss Arden persisted in remaining under his father's protection till his return.

Sicily, the land of fable, was yet unvisited by the travellers. The Count Montalvo, a nobleman of that island, with whom Sir Edward and his nephew were in habits of intimacy, offered to ensure their safety, and become their Cicerone in exploring the many monuments of art and history which that celebrated spot contains. Hypolito was urgent for the tour, as well to escape the observation of a circle with whom he had no pretension to mix, as to indulge his natural taste. The Count had a bark of his own, which, shortly after, conveyed him, with a large party of friends, to Messina. During this little voyage, it was impossible for Hypolito to be wholly invisible; yet the Marquis was hardly less disgusted with his Italian

friends, than his *protégé* declared himself to be.
The rude inquisitive eyes, and broken observations,
of the ill-bred grandees, made both youths happy
to be once more on land. The Marquis had
another reason for avoiding the sea; being always a
severe sufferer by the indisposition it very commonly occasions. When, therefore, the party
proposed visiting the Lipari isles, the Marquis
excused himself, and remained with Hypolito at
the palace of Count Montalvo, who accompanied
Sir Edward. The Prince, then Governor of Messina, ordered in the interval a splendid entertainment, to which the English strangers were
universally invited; nor could the Marquis decline going, though not accustomed to attend these
parties, and very unwilling to leave Hypolito, for
whom his attachment had been daily increasing
in a manner very surprising even to himself.
They had ridden together in the morning, which
proved so sultry, as to have heated the blood of
the Marquis, before he went to the palace of the
prince. A very little excess in wine acted powerfully upon a constitution already feverish with
violent exercise; and he quitted the Governor's
party ere the masqued ball, with which the enter-

tainment was to conclude. The day was not closed when he came home; but Hypolito, who was drawing, had already called for lights. As the Marquis entered the magnificent range of rooms allotted to himself and friends, his eye was led through them all, to the last, where he saw Hypolito deeply engaged with his subject. Shades over the wax-lights softened the glare, and gave the most feminine delicacy to the youth's naturally delicate complexion. His dark locks broke in redundant curls over the fairest forehead in the world, and played upon his throat and neck, the heat having obliged him to throw open his shirt-collar. Suddenly Hypolito took the piece he was drawing, and, holding it behind the light, to survey it, the Marquis could not avoid observing the whiteness and smallness of his hands. " For your own credit, and mine," cried the Marquis, gaily seizing his young favourite by the shoulder, "row, ride, drive, dig — do something to get rid of this white skin, and those delicate hands; for I cannot long stand the raillery I have , encountered for this month past; and you must make up your mind to be considered as a woman in future, unless you contrive to get something more the look' of a man." It was only by chance the Marquis removed his eye from the landscape he had taken from Hypolito, to raise it to his face; but, dropping the drawing from his hands, it there became in a manner riveted. That beauty always too delicate for a man, had now the softest charm of woman; a mantling suffusion a downcast grace. — The dangerous silence that followed, was at length, in a faltering voice, broken by Sir Edward's nephew. "And what embodied angel, then, are you," cried he, "dropt from the skies only to guide and guard me?" — The Marquis spoke in the most winning accent, yet the charmer replied not; but, sinking on his shoulder, as he knelt at her feet, hid there her blushes, and communicated her tremblings. — Let no one vaunt fidelity who avoids not danger. — The Marquis already fevered by wine, found the intoxication now passing into his soul. The fair, the pure image of the distant Marian vanished from his memory; and he saw, heard, thought of, only this nameless, trembling charmer. That she had followed him by choice, was very obvious; — for his sake had indured inconvenience, indignity, fatigue, and even servile degradation. The entreaties which he re-

doubled to extort her secret bewildered more and
more, every moment, a head and heart already
confused and impassioned; nor were the tears
she now profusely poured forth wanting to confirm her influence over the surprised, delighted
lover. How, then, were his feelings awakened, when
she at length avowed herself the slighted daughter
of Sir Edward Arden!—that, hopeless of ever con-
quering in her own character the inveterate prejudice her father owned that he had conceived against
her, and resolved he should never accept her hand
from any motive but choice, she quitted Ireland
before her father and the Marquis left England;
and having assumed this disguise, sought them at
Paris; hardly hoping to escape the keen eye of
her father; but convinced, that if he should recognise her, his pride would make him conceal
an artifice which he would never have authorised.
Happily, however, he had not lived long enough
with her to have the same quick recollection other
parents have of their children. Far, therefore,
from being discovered by him, she had found herself so long overlooked by the Marquis, though
beset by most of his Italian friends, that it was
her full intention, the first safe opportunity, to quit

Messina, and give up all thoughts of a man, who, whether as Miss Arden she sought a lover in him, or as Hypolito a friend, knew not how to distinguish or to value her.

But this was a charge she well knew her own injustice in making : the eyes of the Marquis now dwelt enamoured on her beauty ; his eager ear carried to his heart the comprehensive, though implied tenderness, which her words conveyed. Too well he recollected the slights he had shown Miss Arden ; to atone for them, he knelt, implored, repented, vowed ; *would* be forgiven : — in fine, he was so.   In the ensuing impassioned conversation, nothing occurred that could possibly enlighten the Marquis :- he found this impostor as familiar with his family, — its relations, feelings, secret occurrences, and future prospects, as Miss Arden herself ; and, wholly unsuspicious of the possibility of any deception, indulged the ardour of his nature, and urged her to give him, as the pledge of her forgiveness, that very moment, the hand which alone could ensure it to him.   To surprize Sir Edward on his return, appeared to his nephew a most happy device : the glowing cheek of the fair-one contradicted her words, when

she insisted on waiting the consent of her father.
" Why, why should we?" cried the eager Marquis; " has he not, from the hour of your birth,
bestowed you on the favoured Lenox? Wherefore
sacrifice happiness to form? Now, this very moment, give yourself, my Emily, to a husband,
who will add the remembrance of this generous
condescension to all your virtues and your charms!"
She urged the indelicacy of being married in her
disguise. — It was the only way they could be
married at all, the lover insisted; and they
were in a place where love wore many a disguise. Once let the priest join their hands, and
he pledged his honour to leave her full liberty
to give decorum to her situation, by allowing her
to resume the habit of her sex. Her denials became every moment fainter; and the Marquis,
half inebriated with pleasure, as well as wine,
more importunate. In fine, they stole from the
palace to the great church, where Emily had informed him her confessor officiated; and as he
already knew her secret and its motives, from him
she was aware that no painful objection would be
made respecting her disguise. The priest was
found; two more joined as witnesses, and the

mistaken, impassioned Marquis was solemnly, regularly, married to Emily. — The name of Arden was not mentioned necessarily in the ceremony; and the bridegroom never gave any attention to the certificate he signed, or he would have seen that of Fitzallen subjoined; for it was, indeed, that fiend in human shape, who had thus accomplished the deep revenge which she had so bitterly vowed on Sir Edward and his daughter.

Never, for one moment, had Emily Fitzallen lost sight of the persons whom she was determined to persecute. She followed and discovered the little delicate artifice which Miss Arden had adopted to win the affections of her betrothed husband. That name, that consequence, the gentle Emily thought it wisdom to give up, the vindictive Emily saw she had the power of assuming: and finding when she became the constant companion of the Marquis, that in her own person she might not have influence enough to decide his fate, she resolved to avail herself of the rare advantage of Sir Edward's absence, to borrow his daughter's name: and the unfortunate youth, as if willing to second her views, and destroy his own, had that day allowed his judgment to be obscured, and his constitution inflamed with wine. The priest who performed the marriage ceremony had been previously prepared to attend at a moment's notice, as well as forewarned to be cautious in rendering it full, authentic, and duly witnessed.

The new-married pair found, on returning to the Count's palace, some of his domestics already arrived, to notify the intended landing of the voyagers that evening. The Marquis felt it a respect due to his bride to allow her leisure to resume her own dress, as he had promised; and the increased agitation of mind in which she appeared, claimed this consideration from him.

It would have been much more agreeable to the Marquis, as well as the bride, had the return of their friends been a little deferred. However, as that must happen when it would, the lover was anxious to meet Sir Edward, ere he reached the palace of the Count Montalvo; as well to apprise him of the recent ceremony, as to prepare him to save all three from ridicule by avowing a previous knowledge of his daughter's disguise. Wandering with this view, through those beautiful groves that on all sides border the shores of Messina, the pure air insensibly calmed the spirits, and sobered the brain of the Marquis. He half wished that he had waited the return of his uncle, ere he had wrested from him his daughter; and turned towards the walk on the quay, where he anxiously looked out for the bark of the count. The grandeur and beauty of the view never struck the Marquis so sensibly : behind him arose the magnificent natural semicircle, with the lofty columns of the Palazzata; before him appeared the celebrated strait, once sung by all the Muses; and many of those elegant fictions were yet present to his mind. Blending, in an hour and situation so singular, the romance of poetry with that of love, he threw himself on a marble seat by the fountain of Neptune, and repeated, as he gazed, the verses of Homer.

The blue strait, hardly dimpled by a breeze, was half covered with gaudy galleys, and the boats of fishermen; the fires of the light-house were reflected in glowing undulations on the waves; heavy black clouds, tinged with a dun red, seemed to seek support on the rocky mountains of Calabria; and the winds, after a wild concussion, subsided at once into a horrible kind of stillness. The rowers, whose laborious and lively exertions animate the sea which they people, now made vain, though more vigorous efforts, to take shelter in the harbour. Suddenly the atmosphere became murky and oppressive; the clouds, yet more swoln and dense, sunk so low, that they almost blended with the waters. Not a bird ventured to wing the heavy and unwholesome air; and the exhausted rowers could not catch breath enough to express, by a single cry, the agonising fear that caused cold dews to burst from every pore. A tremendous sense of impending evil seemed to suspend all vital motion in the crowd late so busy around the Marquis; while he himself impulsively partook that sick terror of soul, to which no name has ever yet been given. This awful intuitive sense of the approaching convulsion of nature was, however, only momentary. A tremendous shock followed; the Marquis felt all the danger, and tried to arise; the earth rocked beneath his feet. The marble fountain, near which he rested, was cloven in twain instantaneously; and hardly could he escape the abyss which he saw close over the miserable wretches, who, but a moment before, were standing beside him. Columns of the Palazzata, and other surrounding buildings, fell with a crash, as if the universe were annihilated. The horror yet raged in all its force, when the sudden rise of the earth he stood on, threw the Marquis, and a crowd around him, towards a wall, which must have dashed their brains out, but that, weak as they were, the wall was yet weaker, and fell before them in a cloud of dust. Oh! God, what it was to hear the agonizing shrieks of suffering humanity, blended with the thunders of desolation, and the deep internal groans of disjointed nature! when, to complete the calamities of Messina, the sea, in one moment, burst its bounds; and boiling, as it were, with subterraneous fires, rolled forward, with horrible roarings, a mountainous deluge. As quickly returning, it bore away a train of bruised and helpless wretches; and among them, the man who was so lately the gayest of the gay, the happiest of the happy, — the unfortunate Marquis of Lenox.

Recollection was too fleeting, life too dubious, too fluctuating in the Marquis, when first he found that he was still living, for him to connect his ideas, or utter any sound but sighs and groans. He soon perceived himself to be in a small, but miserable place, encompassed with faces he had never beheld till that moment, while hoarse voices resounded in his ear, equally unknown to him. Alas! the only eye he could have seen with pleasure, dared not meet his; the only voice he could have found comfort in hearing, uttered not a word, lest the agitation, even of pleasure, should, in so weak a state, be death to him.   Yet watching every breath the unfortunate youth drew, ready to echo every groan that burst from him, sat, hid by a curtain, his anxious, his affectionate uncle, Sir Edward Arden: and that the Duke of Aberdeen had yet a son, was rather owing to his natural sensibility, than to his immediate affection.

On the memorable evening of the earthquake at Messina, Sir Edward, the Count Montalvo, and two other Sicilian noblemen, were making the harbour; the sailors having predicted foul weather, though no one suspected the immediate and awful danger impending.   In one moment the mariners, by expressive cries and gestures, made the noblemen comprehend that a singular and frightful motion of the vessel was not natural. Now, as gravitation were, by a strange inversion,

removed to heaven, it was drawn at once back
and upward, then thrown impetuously down into
the dark abyss of the waters, and again in one
moment caught upward, with a reeling, convul-
sive trembling, as if the timber had a vital sense,
and felt the fears of those who would have
governed it, had human art availed against the
struggles of disjointed nature. Yet, tremendous
as was the state of those on the sea, it was safety,
compared to the situation of the sufferers on
land; which the vessel was often thrown so
near, that the horror-struck passengers could
behold the victims on the beach lift up their hands
one moment to heaven for pity, and the next sink
into the burning abyss that opened at their feet.
As no power could steady the bark, or direct its
course, the Count and his friends knew not
whether they, with the helpless mariners who yet
contended hard for life, were to have a watery, or
a flaming grave. Nor was the concussion and
entanglement, with other vessels in the same tremendous predicament, the least of their danger;
though, when thrown out to solitary suffering, that
danger appeared yet more horrible. At this fearful moment every evil was increased, by one of

the prime sailors falling from the mast he was climbing, into the sea. His comrades, with the bold humanity incident to their profession, made the most strenuous efforts to recover him : and one of the sailors fancying, imperfect as the un-natural light was, that he saw the body, leaped overboard with a rope tied under his arms, and was drawn up, clasping a half-drowned wretch, who, it was soon discovered, was not his lost shipmate. Having disengaged this man from the plank he convulsively embraced, and which had, in reality, saved his life, on finding him a mere stranger, the seamen would perhaps have aban-doned him to his fate; but that the fineness of his linen, and a rich watch chain, attracted their attention. In a moment they stript and plundered the insensible sufferer; and the surgeon of the vessel alone saved him from perishing by neglect, who had thus wonderfully escaped the wreck of nature. It is true, his humanity was quickened by the recollection that a man of so delicate an appearance, and who had been as delicately drest, might one day well recompense those who pre-served his life.

Thus, by a strange ordination of things, un-

known and unnoticed, in the poor cabin of the
surgeon, lay, with hardly a symptom of existence,
the Marquis of Lenox; and there, so precarious
was his situation, he might perhaps have expired,
but that the sailors, who had possessed themselves
of his valuables, burnt to convert them into money.
Interest is often the last as well as first principle
in vulgar minds. Hardly had the vessel got out
enough to sea to promise safety, or the elements
subsided sufficiently for the compass to guide,
before a calculation of the plunder was made; and
the watch-seals, with other ornaments of the Marquis, handed among the domestics of the noblemen
for sale. What was the astonishment and horror
of Sir Edward's valet, when he saw to whom they
had so lately belonged! Far from guessing the
fact, he only concluded the man on whom they
were found, to be the murderer of the Marquis,
thus overtaken by the justice of heaven. Instantly
he rushed into the cabin, where Sir Edward and
the noblemen yet remained, stunned, as it were,
with fear and horror. The earthquake was, however, forgotten by Sir Edward in his agony for his
nephew; and not forming the harsh conclusion of
his valet as to the stranger, he demanded to see

the sufferer, that such care might be taken as would preserve his life, and enable him to give all the account in his power of the unfortunate Marquis of Lenox. — What tender anguish overwhelmed Sir Edward, when, wounded, wan, insensible, wrapt in coarse linen, he discovered the dearest object of all his cares, the chief delight of his remaining life — the darling son of his darling sister !

From the surgeon Sir Edward understood, that, besides a great number of bruises, the Marquis had a contusion on the head, attended with a high fever, nor, if it once flew to his brain, could human art save him. The sense of his own danger yet not over — the dreadful images of the horrors he had witnessed — all, all, was lost in the impression made by the beloved object before Sir Edward.— The Marquis was immediately removed to the best bed which the small vessel afforded; every comfort, as well as medicine, anxiously administered : yet many, many miserable days, and sleepless nights, did Sir Edward pass, before he was sure his own life would be prolonged, much less that of an invalid, in so weak a state.

The fever of the Marquis was at length enough

subdued, for Sir Edward to appear by his bedside
— faint ideas of affinity, and tenderness, were
indistinctly afloat in the aching head of the youth,
when his eyes wandered over the features of his
uncle, and in a weak inward voice he murmured
out, " Hypolito." — Sir Edward spoke not, but
raising his eyes to heaven, and letting his hand
fall, implied by this action, that the youth was no
more. — Intense faintings, and convulsions, seized
the Marquis. The relapse was so alarming that
he had been many days in a palace at Naples, and
attended by the ambassador's physician, before he
was allowed again to behold a face that might
once more confuse those faculties on which it was
plain his existence depended. — Yet no sooner did
the interesting affectionate eyes of his uncle meet
his, than he again sighed out, " Oh ! Sir, Hypolito !" — " That we have life ourselves, my dear
Lenox," returned Sir Edward, " is little less than
a miracle: — to preserve yours, you must be
patient, silent, submissive — need I say, that you
have not a wish I would not anticipate — a feeling
I would not spare? Imagine every thing said you
would have said — every thing done you would
have done.

Alas ! of the most generous assiduity the Marquis was well assured ; and this it was struck so deep a despair through his heart.   The sad history of the affinity the lost Hypolito bore to Sir Edward, was yet in the bosom of her lover ; and no other being knew at what an interesting moment the disguised fair one had been so awfully inhumed.   In the delirium which attended his fever, Sir Edward had, with great surprise, heard his nephew now call for Hypolito, now for Emily — now for Marian — now urge a disguised beauty to an immediate marriage ; and smile at the scruples she made to decide her fate without her father's being present, when "it would make Sir Edward so happy to find her a bride." These vague rhapsodies applied so exactly to the disguise, the passion, and the secret situation of the Marquis, with Sir Edward's daughter, that the only conclusion that tender father drew from these complicated wanderings and incoherent expressions was, that Emily had, in spite of all her promises, betrayed her own secret to her lover.   How sad and dear was the delight of thinking, then, that even in delirium she was the only object who existed to that lover.

Time, however, strengthened the intellects, and improved the health of the Marquis, who then learnt the melancholy consequences of that earthquake, which, by throwing him into the sea, had in fact preserved his life. He dared not flatter himself that his bride had alike escaped; for, it was too sure she would have eagerly sought her father and her husband; and how should he be able to disclose the tremendous secret of her fate? Should *he* afflict the generous uncle who lived but in his looks, by telling him, that the very moment which accomplished his wishes had snatched away the dearer object of them? No; better was it that Sir Edward should still suppose Miss Arden living under the Duke's protection, and waiting their return.

The Marquis was at an age when the spirits make great efforts to rise above the calamities of life. However strong the impression made by the lovely disguised fair one, however tender and sacred the tie that bound him to her, the impression was sudden, the tie incomplete. Sir Edward judged it wise to assume such a general cheerfulness as might renovate his nephew's spirits; and the attempt insensibly dissipated the gloom

and horror that for some time hung about the
young man. The soft, the soothing remembrance
of the fair, the gentle Marian, now daily recurred.
Marian yet lived — lived too for him; nor would
ever know his generous infidelity — an infidelity
which the grateful affection he felt for his uncle
almost sanctified; and which, having swayed him
to fulfil a dear and sacred duty (for thus frail mor-
tals extenuate to themselves their lapses), no
longer obliged him to forego the cherished choice
of his heart. During the term of his nephew's
sickness and convalescence, Sir Edward had kept
back several letters of his daughter, which now
were delivered to her lover in a packet; and the
Marquis drew thence a renovating power, which
not even the pure air of Naples could afford.

In the long leisure of a sick chamber, the Marquis had often pondered over the extraordinary
situation from which he had so miraculously escaped with life; and though there remained not a
hope that Hypolito survived, (for why, in that case,
did he not appear?) an ardent wish lived in the
mind of the widower bridegroom once more to revisit the memorable scene of his marriage — to
learn, if possible, the manner and moment of the

death of the disguised fair one — to see at least the priest who had, in an hour teeming with horror and evil, united their hands — to shed before him some tears of generous anguish — and, in the great church at Messina, to consecrate the memory of the unfortunate Emily, by a magnificent monument.

The danger of revisiting Sicily had now for some time been over; and when Sir Edward found his nephew strenuous in the wish, he no longer opposed, though he did not choose to accompany him. A bark was engaged by the melancholy Marquis, who, passing many a scene of desolation, at length sailed into the almost choked-up harbour of Messina; an awful memento of the vain labours of man, and all the little pride of human magnificence. The half-fallen pier — the tottering Palazzata — the solitary strand, and the indistinct streets, through which crawled a few mangled wretches, who lived only to envy those whom the earth had wholly swallowed up, — made the very soul of the Marquis recoil within him before he reached the great church, and convent adjoining. An enormous mass of ruins alone marked the spot where they once stood. Of the priest he sought, not a trace remained. The whole brotherhood had vanished, either into a premature grave, or in search of a remote, but safe home. The bare walls of the palace of Count Montalvo, though injured, had not fallen, but it was plundered of the magnificent furniture, nor inhabited by a single domestic. In fine, no being remained in Messina whom the Marquis had ever seen there, nor was the unhappy stranger he inquired for known, either by description or name. How could an individual be remembered in a place where society was become an echo, and the grandeur of ages annihilated by a single convulsion in nature? The Marquis again slowly and sadly ascended his bark, and, casting his eyes over the ravaged glories of Messina, " Ah ! why, my Emily," sighed he, " when I have so awful a proof how vain is the busy pride of mortality, should I attempt to raise a monument to thee? The God who at such a moment, and in such a manner, claimed thee, has made Messina thine !" Then turning appalled from the enormous mass of splendid ruins, he hastily cut through the green waves, on which the evening sun still played with undiminished, unaltered beauty.

Again in Naples, the Marquis, though silent and melancholy, was not inconsolable. During his convalescence, he had rather felt, than seen, his boundless influence over his uncle; which it was now his first wish to increase; that when the day came for him to acknowledge the humble choice his heart had made, he might act on a nature so generous, in favour of his lovely, his interesting Marian. It was the subject of great surprise to him, that Miss Arden's singular disappearance should be yet a secret to her father: but, as Sir Edward had long forborne to mention her from prudence, and the Marquis always avoided it from choice, this was not a moment to lead to so painful a disclosure by a single question. Too soon would it be, whenever a father so tender learnt her melancholy fate. It must then become *his* duty and choice alike to sooth and to console his uncle. Perhaps, when the bitterness of grief was assuaged, and Sir Edward learnt the sacred rite which brought them still nearer in affinity than nature had, that generous man might in turn

be brought to adopt, and second, the only feeling
that could induce him to take another bride. —
If so, why should he prolong his banishment?
His own country now contained not the once
dreaded Miss Arden, while in that country lived
for him, and him alone, his Marian.

After a term of apparent weariness and constraint, the Marquis one day abruptly proposed to
his uncle returning to England. The keen, but
delighted eye of Sir Edward, seemed to pierce his
very soul; yet vainly did he seek to account for
the cloud that immediately succeeded on the brow
of the Marquis, or a kind of stifled compassion for
himself that followed the proposition. No possible
objection to it, however, occurred upon the part
of Sir Edward; on the contrary, a gay flow of
spirits, extremely embarrassing and distressing to
his nephew. The youth found himself almost
unable to keep the dreadful secret; but having
long seen, in all the gay scenes of Italy, only the
grave of Sir Edward's lovely and affectionate
daughter, he could not controul his increasing
impatience to depart directly; yet urged his weak
health, as rendering it necessary he should travel
very leisurely, a mode which he knew his uncle

detested. Having settled his route, and appointed
to join each other in Switzerland, he left Sir
Edward to fulfil some excursive engagements, and
set out, attended only by his servants.

Gentle exercise, pure air, the variety of simple
scenes and objects around him, gradually invigorated the health of the Marquis, and made him
delight to linger in Switzerland. Who would not
delight to linger in Switzerland? Who would not
wish the soul now to dilate into grandeur, and
now, with sweet compression, to contract into
content, as majestic or simple nature takes its turn
to act upon it? — In that wild region our traveller
found all the fervor of romantic passion rekindled
in his soul. He walked till he could walk no
longer; — he rested only to gain strength to walk
again: — and, if fatigue caused him to sleep, he
carried into the torpor necessary to repair exhausted nature, rich and fanciful visions, not less
delightful than those he cherished when awake.
Nevertheless, a carriage and led horse accompanied our pedestrian; for such had been the
orders of his father. — The carriage he was often
pleased to fill with tired and rosy vintagers, on
whose gratitude he made no demand. His horse

frequently lightened the way to the sun-burnt
veteran, who sought,

——————— " When all his toils were past,
" Still to return, and die at home at last."

The Marquis, thus generously employing his
superfluous advantages, would delight to linger
behind; resting under the shadow of some grotesque
mountain, and listening to the dashing of some
distant water-fall, while his mind now solemnly
paused upon the past, now fondly mused on the
uncertain future.

After a day passed in this luxurious manner,
night so suddenly surprised the Marquis, in a
solitary but beautiful valley some miles from Lausanne, that, had not his servants, apprehending
him to be too ill, or too much exhausted, to come
on, returned with the carriage, he must have slept
upon the grass. Once within it, he indulged the
slumber fatigue occasioned, and had been well
shaken by his valet, before he could be sufficiently
roused to understand that his chaise was stopt by
another, overturned in the road, and so broken,
that the lady and her maid were hopeless of reaching Lausanne, unless some benevolent traveller
would either assist to repair the mutilated equi-

page, or accommodate them with his own. The Marquis, a little cross at having so comfortable a nap interrupted, did not find himself in the humour to alight. Nevertheless, he sent in his own name a polite though unwilling offer of his carriage, but did not think the stranger too complaisant in immediately accepting it. This, however, left him no choice but to spring out, and show his involuntary knight-errantry. The hills on each side were covered with wood, which, meeting over the road, added darkness to the night. Having, though with difficulty, got his carriage safely past the broken one, the Marquis, with great gallantry, handed in two trembling females, who seemed hardly able to thank him ; and having given the postillions strict charge of them, returned to survey the shattered equipage : his valet being provided with phosphoric matches, by which he lit a taper. After various proposals to tie it together, the Marquis thought its appearance so unsafe, that, tired as he was, he chose to mount a horse, and follow his own carriage, which was not yet out of hearing. · He was near enough to the inn when the strangers alighted to have offered his assistance ; but a little disgusted with the want of

consideration on their parts, and perceiving, by
the candles held at the door, that his hands and
clothes were covered with dust, he thought it a
respect due to himself, rather than the stranger,
to rectify his appearance.   To dress never took
the Marquis much time; and to his request to
inquire after the lady's health an immediate permission was accorded.   As he had sent in his
name, the landlord stood ready with lights to
precede " *Milor Anglois*" into the apartment of
the stranger.

As the Marquis glanced his quick eye forward,
he observed that the lady had, like himself, recti-
fied her dress: for leaning one arm gracefully on
a low old-fashioned slab, and with the other caressing a beautiful Italian greyhound, stood a female,
at once so slight, graceful, and dignified, as to
rivet his attention, and give a strange, wild, pro-
phetic pulsation to his heart.   This elegant traveller had the air of high rank, affluence, and
fashion.   She was wrapt in a riding robe of black
velvet, lined with white satin, and girt to her
waist by a cord of silver.   A pale blue velvet
hat, with a plume of white feathers, was thrown
carelessly on one side, yet tied under her chin by

a white and silver handkerchief. Over the black velvet robe fell, in vast profusion, rich curls of fair hair, from which the Marquis, by a kind of intuitive conviction, seemed to recognize the fair Italian; while the whole graceful figure announced to him his Marian. Nor did he err in either instance: the charmer turned towards him, and he saw — not the humble daughter of Dennis, though every feature of Marian. Ah! no, this was, and was not, Marian; — an elegant, conscious, high-bred beauty, now stood before him: yet, in the chastened delight with which her eye surveyed him, he read the triumph of his own. How new — how tumultous were his emotions! how exquisite, yet agonising, the embrace she denied not! That Marian was distinguished, her lover plainly saw — that she might be infamous, he severely felt. Yet, such is the contrariety of human emotions, that the tears in which his eyes swam, sprang more from perceiving her to be independent of himself than a juster cause. The air of this irresistible charmer, however, was not more tender than it was innocent. She blushed, it is true; but it seemed to be only for the distress she occasioned; since she hardly knew how to interpret that agitation which the Marquis attempted not to controul. "I have surprised you, my Lord," faltered she: then, sweetly smiling, added, "and I too have been in turn surprised." — "The meeting with my Marian," replied her lover, again fondly clasping her, "would be a pleasure past all speaking; *but*" — "But what, my Lord?" — "To find her *thus!*" — the Marquis cast his eyes over her dress. "Oh! is that all your distress?" cried she, with a glow of triumphant pleasure; "I will not be my own historian, positively, when there is a better at hand: let Sir Edward Arden be summoned to expound the mystery." — "Sir Edward Arden, my angel, is far from hence; and my Marian must, in pity of the heart wholly her own, expound this mystery herself." — "Nay, my Lord," playfully and in exultation returned the charmer, "I may hazard much with *you* in the avowal of my name; but nothing with Sir Edward Arden, by demanding in his arms a welcome for his wandering daughter."

The concussion of nature that swallowed up the impostor Hypolito could alone equal that which now shook the mental system of the Marquis. Yet a single thought was conclusive; a single impulse conviction.   Yes, the gracious, the graceful creature, now bending benignly to raise him from the earth where his misery had laid him, was, could be, only the angel daughter of Sir Edward; the being, formed and finished, " the cunning'st pattern of excelling nature;" who, whether as a masqued Italian Grace, a rustic maid, or a high-bred beauty, was intuitively adored by him, and claimed in his heart, whatever shape she wore, a rightful sovereignty. But whence then came the arch-fiend to whom he had at Messina plighted his hand? No doubt from the hell that opened to swallow her, ere yet the sin was consummated. — How, how, unless endued with supernatural knowledge, could any female but Sir Edward's daughter have discussed with him the many secret domestic occurrences of both their families, which were not more familiar, as it appeared, to his mind, than hers?

And well might this bewilder the ideas of the unhappy Marquis, who had never been enough a party in the little history of Miss Arden to learn that a creature like Emily Fitzallen even existed; — still less that this companion of her infancy had ungratefully supplanted her, and then vowed

K 2

a bitter revenge, which she had, alas! too successfully executed.

That delicate pride which nature makes one
of the first charms of woman was a little wounded
in Emily Arden, on observing a revulsion of soul
so singular in the Marquis.   Yet it was plain he
suffered much ; so deadly a paleness lived on his
cheek, so melting a sadness marked his voice,
that, unintelligible as the cause remained (for he
answered not to her fondest entreaties), so tender
was her heart, and the lover at her feet so entirely
the object of its tenderness, as to make her lose
every other anxiety in that of consoling him.
Too true was the sympathy for her to attempt it
in vain : their hearts were formed for each other,
and, without a single vow, united. Hypolito, in
a moment of such exquisite felicity, as completely vanished from the recollection of the
Marquis, as if the impostor had never existed.
Sir Edward Arden was no longer missed by his
daughter; and two whole happy hours elapsed in
endearment and protestation ere Miss Arden remembered that she was faint for want of food, or
the Marquis that he was dying with fatigue, when
they met.   But was ever repast more delicious

than the humble one to which they sat down, when mutual love thus graced and blest the board? How playfully did the Marquis arraign the inflexibility of the fair one, who commanded him to recover his good looks by the morning, when from the table she early past to a chamber, where the sweet consciousness of rewarded virtue hallowed the slumbers of the amiable Emily.

Not alike pure and unbroken was the rest of the Marquis; so strange, so singular was his situation, so inexplicable his recollections, that he found it impossible to regulate his feelings or calm his spirits. To his distempered fancy the chamber rocked with the earthquake of Sicily one moment, and the next was illuminated with the visible presence of a guardian angel, in the form of his adored Emily: nor were his slumbers more peaceful; marriage and death by turns seemed to demand a victim; and glad was he to see that day break which restored to his eyes and heart the beloved object, who alone could chase away each painful thought.

But what a day of delight arose to Miss Arden! at last to see herself the sole hope of the man who ruled her very fate. Now no longer under the painful necessity of concealment, shunned, dreaded, abhorred, the remembrance that she once had been so, only gave sweet confirmation of her power, and exalted happiness into triumph. She was told her father was coming to meet her; and though well she knew the share he would take in the transport, she found it most perfect without him. Safe in her lover's protection, she felt for the first time the fond pleasure of solely depending on him.

The Marquis, on the contrary, counted the hours till his uncle should arrive; for from his hand alone could he hope to receive that of Miss Arden: and dear as was the heart she gave him, he felt it to be only part of an invaluable treasure, wholly destined for himself.

A simple train of circumstances had produced this romantic meeting of the lovers. The awful escape of the Marquis at Messina left him in a state of such danger, that Sir Edward could not conceal it entirely from the Duke; though he forbore, as long as possible, the communication, in hopes of some favourable turn. The Duke, impetuous as his son in all his feelings, forgot how acutely Miss Arden would sympathise, and almost killed her with the dreadful recital of her father. To fly to the beloved of her heart, to watch over, cherish, soothe, recover, or perish with him, was Emily's first thought, and, indeed, her only one. The alarm of the Duke left her without a doubt of his setting out for Italy on the arrival of the next letter; and hardly could the afflicted Emily breathe till it came. That letter bringing, however, better accounts of the Marquis, the Duke coolly left him to the care of his uncle, and thought, from that moment, once more only of himself and his libertine indulgences. Plunged in grief, shut up from company, yet disgusted with her home, Emily soon was shocked with discovering it to be an improper one. The Duke was either less attentive than usual to the respect due to Miss Arden, or she found her preception quickened by the desire she felt to be gone; but it was impossible for her to misunderstand the terms on which the Duke, and the widow, engaged to give propriety to the young lady's residence in his house, now lived. The disgust and shame of such an affront, however, was soon lost in the recollection that it authorised Emily to follow her own inclinations, and seek her father. She soon found occasion so express her dissatisfaction at the conduct of the *lady*, without seeming to include the Duke in the censure ; and announced her intention of availing herself of the return of Sir Edward's courier, who might, with her own suite, conduct her to Italy. The Duke took no pains to investigate, much less over-rule, a resolution which left him peaceful possession of his mistress, and his own mansion; but allowed Miss Arden to stay or go, as she should think most eligible. On mature deliberation Emily persuaded herself (so fallacious, are our reasonings where the heart is impressed) that to run over the continent in search of her father, — for she never allowed her lover to appear a part of her consideration, — was absolutely an act of discretion, and accordingly took leave of the Duke.

When once on the road, the impatience which Miss Arden could not restrain showed too plainly the tender motive of her journey. Having agreed to rest in Switzerland, merely till Sir Edward's servant should notify her approach, she had sent him forward only a single day, when the breaking down of her carriage prevented her passing, in the dark, the very person she sought.

The delightful rambles of two lovers through that delightful country may easily be imagined. Sir Edward lost no time, from the moment his servant reached him, in hurrying to meet his daughter ; wondering much at every town that he saw her not.—— But where could it be such happiness to see her, as leaning, with frank affection, on the arm of his nephew, while the glad eyes of both hailed him as the author, the partaker of their felicity? This was, indeed, all of joy a father can know : — to behold his Emily, at last, sweetly conscious of absolute power, yet using it only to give delight : — to hear the nephew, whom he had ever loved with parental fondness, implore absolution from him, for the sins of ingratitude and perverseness, while both, with tender, anxious eyes, demanded from his hand each other. Where could three beings be found so much to be envied? Yet, of these three, the father knew, perhaps, the most exquisite felicity ; for he had known the most torturing doubts.

The Marquis, impatient in all things, was for being married the very next day; but this, Sir Edward urged, was, from a variety of causes, impossible. Miss Arden's fortune would then be

too much in the Duke's power; who, perhaps,
loved himself well enough, poorly to leave his son,
during a life that promised continuance, dependent
on his wife.   So mortifying a suggestion silenced
the Marquis, but made him alike urgent to proceed directly to England, where all these arrangements could most expeditiously be made.   And
now the gentle Emily became the objector ; she
could not, truly, leave unseen the beauties of Italy,
nor was troubled with the least fear for her fortune.
All necessary points might, she observed, be settled quite as well without their presence : in short,
her father easily comprehended that Miss Arden
feared, in returning unmarried, she should be exposed to the ridicule of having come abroad to
seek a tardy lover ; or rather, that she veiled, under
this idea, the same determination with the Marquis ; and both were alike ready to be united. Sir
Edward, therefore, once more dispatched his servant to England, with such proposals to the Duke
as he thought eligible ; and only required of the
lovers to accompany him to Naples, where, on the
arrival of the settlements, they could be publicly
married in the chapel of the English embassador ;
after which Emily might, without impropriety,

accompany them to Rome. The Marquis was perfectly easy on every point, but the tedious time which must necessarily elapse : as Sir Edward, however, during the journey, almost always chose to ride his nephew's horse, and give up his seat in the chaise to him, the lovers contrived to pass the interval pleasantly enough.

The reason which Sir Edward gave for delaying the marriage was so prudent, that it easily imposed upon the Marquis, but not on Miss Arden. She had penetrated too deeply into her father's character not to perceive that pride was his foible ; and, by the refinement of his nature, she had always been his pride. Sensible that he was born to give way to his nephew himself, it was only by holding his daughter high he could render it obvious that she was not elevated by marrying her cousin. In the splendor of the union, the fond father sought to give an addition to happiness ; — the hearts of the lovers told them that was not to be given.

The courier, dispatched to England to await the drawing up due settlements under the auspices of the Duke, could not so soon return, but that the party had ample leisure to visit the classical scenes around Naples, in all the intoxication of youth, love, curiosity, and pleasure. Yet fits of absence and gloom, wholly unintelligible to his fair mistress, frequently came over the Marquis; and the name of Hypolito often trembled on his lips, although it never escaped them. How should he resolve to debase himself so far, as to tell his adored Emily, that an impostor, infamous for aught he knew, had so successfully assumed her name and character, as to impress herself upon his heart, and decide his fate? or even, if he might venture to rely on her forgiveness, was it possible he should admit to his uncle that he had been made so egregious a dupe?

Sir Edward understanding too well one cause of his nephew's melancholy and abstracted air, now apprised his daughter of the history and deplorable fate of Hypolito; whom he spoke of so partially, that Emily wept for the loss which the Marquis must long feel of such an accomplished, attached associate. Warned, however, by her father, that to appear to know the sorrow of her lover would be to cherish it, she employed all the charms she well knew how to render successful, to inspirit the Marquis; nor would ever suffer the

conversation to turn toward Sicily, or an earthquake. Yet, in the exquisite sense of power and
passion, she sometimes envied the lost Hypolito,
even in the grave, his influence over the heart
where she should exclusively have reigned.

A palace and establishment, suitable to her fortune, having been provided in Naples for Miss
Arden, her father and the Marquis contented
themselves with their former home. The lady of
the English embassador was distantly allied to
the Bellarney family, and soon circulated the reason of the obvious difference in Sir Edward's mode
of living and his daughter's. She introduced Miss
Arden at court, who was thought so irresistible,
that hardly had the Marquis a friend who was not
secretly his rival. Sir Edward triumphed in the
admiration his daughter excited; but she loved
too truly not to blush at pleasing any man, except him it was her duty, as well as choice, to
please. Often did she sigh at the vain parade
of her almost empty palace, when she saw its
gates close every evening upon her father and her
lover; nor had she any consolation for the tedious etiquette by which she was enslaved, but

that of knowing the arrival of the courier from England would end it.

Sir Edward's servant at length returned, and the Marquis had the gratification of finding that his uncle had not been just in the idea he formed of his father. The Duke of Aberdeen very liberally assigned to his son, during his own life, a third of the estates which he would wholly inherit; and to Miss Arden made over, with the concurrence of the Marquis, for the term of hers, all her own possessions, settling them on the younger children of the marriage, to be alloted at the joint pleasure of the father and mother. To this the Duke added letters equally kind and polite, with the promise of a splendid set of jewels to the bride.

There being no longer any cause for delay, the evening of the next day was fixed for the nuptials, which the English embassador claimed the honour of witnessing, with his lady, in his own chapel; nor would he excuse the party from supping *al fresco* in his gardens.

The happy morning at length arrived; and the Marquis, having ordered a gay *divertissement,* came to the hotel of Miss Arden to breakfast. The performers were all stopt in the hall, and the lover only admitted to the garden: where, as by magic, had arisen a straw-roofed cottage, in which appeared, in the simple garb of Scotland, the affianced bride; while, by her, in a habit humble as that of Dennis, stood her real father. The repast was in the same plain style; and had not the fragrant tuberose, and flowering orange, scented the air, the delighted Marquis would have thought himself still in his native shades — those sweet solitudes, where first his heart expanded to love and happiness.

The more brilliant entertainment of music which the lover had prepared, was given afterwards; but to the masquers was added the fair-haired Italian peasant, whose light fingers once more swept the mandoline with inimitable grace. That pleasure past, Emily again vanished, but soon to return in the chaste elegance of her bridal dress. Long robes of white muslin, spangled with silver, were girt to her waist by a zone of purple, clasped with rich diamonds. The redundance of her locks was a little confined, by part of them being braided with glowing purple, and strings of pearl, without

any other ornament. Several bracelets of pearl
encircled her polished and snowy arms, the beauty
of which never was so obvious, as while her father, holding one hand, and her lover the other,
conducted her up through the portico of the embassador's palace. At the gate, the party were
met by the noble owner and his lady, who usher-
ed them through a magnificent gallery to the
chapel. It was splendidly illuminated, and so
gaily decorated with festoons of roses, as to appear, indeed, the temple of Hymen. Sir Edward
Arden, in the fullness of delight, now fixed his
eyes on those of his beloved nephew, and now on
the downcast lids of his daughter, and saw, in the
arrival of this moment, every wish he had ever
formed, accomplished. The chaplain began the
solemn service; and Sir Edward, taking the two
hands so dear to him, in the presence of God and
man, joined the pair whom he once thought no
time, no chance, would ever unite. In the gardens of the palace, a splendid collation was soon
afterwards served, and an invisible concert prolonged the tedious time to the Marquis, who
watched the glance of Sir Edward's eye, to lead
home his Emily — his own dear Emily. During

the interval, the palace had been universally illuminated, and a great crowd had assembled on the steps of the portico. Distressed at becoming in such a moment the sole object of attention, Emily, in descending, stumbled. The bridegroom, concluding that some one had trod upon her robe, turned hastily round to disengage it, and fixed his eyes on those of—Hypolito. Yes, the ghastly phantom appeared in the very same boyish habiliments which he wore when the Marquis last beheld him: and, oh! fatal memento of their tremendous meeting, and yet more tremendous parting, held up in full view the ring, the fatal ring, with which the unfortunate youth had wedded the fair, the fascinating impostor. It had been one of his mother's, hastily applied, however ill-suited to this purpose; but it was too remarkable to be mistaken; nor could the wretched gazer doubt its identity. The exquisite vision of love, hope, and happiness, faded at once from the soul of the agonized bridegroom; and he sunk, a corpse in appearance, at the feet of the trembling daughter of Sir Edward Arden.

The portico resounded with the cries of the sorrowful and astonished spectators. The Mar-

quis was carried into the nearest apartment, and a
medical gentleman immediately lanced a vein in
his arm. Wan, as though arising from the grave,
the lover at length opened his eyes, and, wildly
glancing them around, no longer allowed them to
dwell on her so lately their sole object; but,
hardly permitting the surgeon time to bind up the
orifice, sprang with the strength of a lunatic from
those who encircled him, to fly through the ar-
cade — traverse the chapel — the illuminated gal-
leries — from thence, in the desperation of sudden
frenzy, he rushed down the steps of the portico —
but too certain, at length, that the object of his
search was no longer visible, he struck his head
against a marble pillar with such force as to stun
himself. Sir Edward Arden, hardly less frantic at
a misery so wholly unintelligible, directed his
servants to lift his nephew into his coach, and
carry him back to the hotel they both inhabited.
A trembling hand seized the arm of Sir Edward;
and the pale face of his Emily anxiously explored
his, while repeating, "The Marquis, my father,
has now a house of his own — it is your Emily
who must henceforward entreat for a home with
her husband." Conscious of she knew not what

violation of decorum in this, she sweetly shrunk
from his glance, and blushed : yet in a moment

>   —— " A thousand innocent shames
> " In angel-whiteness bore away those blushes."

Pressing his tender Emily to his bosom, Sir Edward
dropt on hers tears of infantine softness and affection. " Sweetest of creatures," cried he, " hardly can this unhappy young man be termed thy
husband." " Have I not even now called on
Heaven and man, my father, to witness the vow
that long, long since, wedded my soul to his?
Yes, Edward, beloved Edward," cried she, turning with a gush of tears to the still insensible
bridegroom, " I am thine — for ever thine! Sick
or well, happy or miserable, thy Emily feels it the
dear, sad duty of her life, to watch over, sooth,
sustain thee. The grave alone, perhaps not even
that, can sever from thine the soul now repeating
the fond, unalienable vow, to him who is, alas!
no longer able to return it."

Sir Edward made no further opposition to the
wish of his daughter; and the bridal hours were
past by the tender agitated Emily in anxious
watchings. A raging fever followed the horrible
convulsion of mind which the Marquis had under-

gone: in its paroxysms the affrighted bride a
thousand times heard him renounce, abhor, the vow
of marriage, by which " he had allied himself to
perdition." Starting up with fearful glaring eyes, he
would command her to quit his sight — never,
never more, to appear before him. The frenzy,
then, would be illumined with a ray of reason; he
suddenly beheld in her a benignant angel, de-
scended to save him from the horrors of his own
soul. — He would, with that tenderness which was
ever so successful, implore her *never* to quit his
bed-side — *never* once to take from his eyes those
charming ones which alone could soften his sufferings; and now pressing her hand to his throbbing
temples, and now to his burning bosom, seem to
think it quieted each dangerous pulsation; and
thus, at intervals, lulled himself into the stupefaction which gave him strength again to struggle.
From the imperfect slumbers into which her fondness soothed him, he would again start with con-
vulsive shudderings — insist that the room rocked
with an earthquake; that the sun was turned into
blood — heap dreadful curses on an Emily,
" loathsome to his eyes, and fatal to his honour"
— demand in wild transports " the ring, the fatal

ring, with which *the fiend had enchained his very soul ;"* — and, when the agonised daughter of Sir Edward Arden hastily drew off the one which he had so lately given her, to present it to him, he would gaze mournfully on that, and mysteriously on her — then cry, " No, no !" — wander through faint recollections, and, gently replacing the bond of dear affiance, draw fondly towards him the heart-broken Emily, and deluge her bosom with his tears.

Sacred is the bond of calamity, when thus the visitation comes from Heaven. Could Emily in the arms of the Marquis have known so dear a tenderness as that she felt when hovering near his sick-bed, conscious that he existed but by the love that would willingly have made him immortal? When did any pleasure of sense equal that with which the almost expiring lover took from her eyes, and from her hand, the daily portion of prolonged existence?

Sir Edward shared in the assiduities of his daughter, when the Marquis began to recover. Yet a strange apprehension, in spite of his better reason, too often presented itself to his mind, which Emily knew not: he saw, or fancied he saw, that as the strength and spirits of the Marquis returned, he found their company an oppression. Alas! the tender father was not mistaken. What tortures of mind succeeded the sufferings of body, from which the miserable Lenox at last escaped! He knew the only good on earth which his soul desired to be his own, yet found himself not the richer. Could he, in the fatal circumstance he stood in, dare to sully the purity of his angel Emily? Too well he knew the ring she wore gave him no claim to her endearing tenderness — would convey no inheritance to her children — nay might, by the malice of a fiend, be taken from her finger. To the fury of fever, and frenzy, now succeeded a sullen, settled, impenetrable despair. If he appeared at all, his eyes were haggard, his hair dishevelled; he hardly sat a moment at the table — forgot he was desired to eat — and, strangely departing from all the civilities of life, no less than its social feelings, would often rush from the room, to shut himself up again in his own apartment. Nor was that apartment any longer accessible to the miserable Emily. Yet hours and hours she waited anxiously in the ante-chamber, while he paced irregularly in the one within.

Alas! the sighs and groans that at intervals escaped him pierced her very soul,

Sir Edward Arden now too sensibly felt how incompetent we are to judge of that which we so boldly demand of Heaven as happiness. A thousand times the Marquis had, with the energetic delight of a lover, told him he adored his daughter : he could not but see that she lived in the looks of his nephew. It had been the pride, the pleasure of his life, to give them to each other ; yet not one of the three found, in the accomplishment of this only wish, felicity.

Not from his daughter, however, could Sir Edward draw a breath of complaint. It was her wan cheek, when she was no longer permitted to watch over her husband, — it was the faint flutter, and delicate glow, that teinted her complexion, when he appeared, — it was the tears she stifled in his presence, but that flooded her eyes whenever he vanished, which alone told to her fond father the painful sense she had of so deep an unkindness. A thousand times Sir Edward resolved to inquire into the motives of his nephew's total estrangement — as often the apprehensive Emily left him nothing to complain of, by taking on herself the fault; and insisting, that time, and time only, would enable her to recover the shock and fatigue of so long an attendance on so alarming a malady — confess an obligation to the Marquis for returning her kindness, in allowing her to do as she pleased; and finally, with a delicate address, conveyed through her father this to her husband. What was her grief and astonishment, to find that this information contributed more to tranquillize his mind than all her cares had done! The fatal idea, that she had been from the first deceived, and he had married her only for her fortune, then suddenly forced itself upon her. No sooner did the Marquis begin to ride abroad, and resume his usual habits of life, than the deserted Emily shut herself up in her own apartment, and almost died at so marked, so cruel a neglect.

Ah! could she have known the employment — the sole employment of the man whom she distrusted, — every moment of his absence was spent in searching for that fiend, whom, once found, he hoped to sooth, or bribe, to allow of the annulling of a marriage certainly incomplete, but which only her acknowledgment could prove so. That obtained, he meant to throw himself at the feet of Sir Edward's daughter; and, by confessing the whole truth, prove what appeared to be his fault, was in reality his virtue — the daring to shun the bride whose tenderness he returned with adoration.

The search, the inquiries of the hapless husband, availed not: this fearful phantom, at whose presence virtue and happiness at once vanished, having completed that object, seemed ever to sink into the hell that alone could have engendered her. After a thousand struggles to reconcile his feelings with his conscience, the Marquis found he must still shun his Emily, and, by returning immediately to London, have the advice of the civilians there on the possibility of annulling the first marriage, and making the second valid.

But the latter object, it soon seemed probable, the Marquis need not strive so assiduously to attain: it appeared to himself, as well as to the distracted father, a dreadful doubt, whether Emily would live to see England again. A grief, too severe for medicine to cure, had already made deep ravages on the constitution of the Marchioness. Her heart, thrown back upon her

hands, chilled the pure bosom it returned to.
The hours usually devoted to rest were spent by
her in vain conjectures concerning her husband,
to whom she naturally imputed some other attachment.   Yet still, in company, his eyes were ever
fixed on her with a dying fondness, though he
sought her not at any other time.   Determined
to fulfil her duty, even in the extreme, Emily
exhausted herself in efforts to please, or to amuse
him.   She played, she drew enchantingly.   She
charmed all who came within her circle, and often
saw, in the pride which the Marquis indulged
whenever she was admired, that fond appropriation
of herself, wholly irreconcileable with his painful
neglect.

The physician having declared the Marchioness
in too precarious a state of health to venture a
long journey, proposed her leaving Naples for a
more retired situation.   A villa was easily procured; and her father, unable to endure the inexplicable vexation, made an excursion to Rome,
to endeavour to beguile, in the society of the wise
and lettered men of that city, the deep chagrin of
which he saw no probable end.

He had the little relief of shortly after hearing,

from Emily, that the sweet spot she lived in had revived her spirits, and amended her health. Each letter gave him more cheerful accounts. Not only his daughter, but the Marquis, at length implored him to return, and both joined in assuring him that his presence, his paternal presence, alone was wanting to their happiness. This assurance had too often reached Sir Edward's ears, while only misery was before his eyes, for him to give much credit to it; but the anxious desire he had to know whether his daughter's health was really restored, made him at length risk visiting the infatuated pair, whom wedlock, as it seemed, alone could alienate. But they were alienated no longer; every trace of vexation and sickness had so entirely vanished, that it was only by his memory Sir Edward could assure himself either had existed. In perfect harmony with each other, the married lovers diffused over the beautiful spot they inhabited the charms of paradise itself: for what were they but innocence and love? was the Marquis then innocent? — fain, fain, would he believe so. The angel Emily, who lived *for,* lived *with* him, and was perhaps too charming always to be withstood. Her image so

wholly occupied his soul, that the horrible one of
Hypolito became at length faint, indistinct, aërial
— it was the interest of the hapless lover to persuade himself, that the heart-harrowing form, holding the ring on the steps of the embassador's palace, was shaped by his fancy merely : and the
variety of frightful visions, which impressed his
brain in the progress of his fever, had assumed figures so various and distorted, that well might
he doubt whether fear had not conjured up the
formidable phantom which at that interesting
moment shook his nature.   So fruitless too had
been his after-search, that he at length fondly flattered himself the object of it no longer
existed; and it was not the dead, but the living,
whom the unhappy Lenox was born to dread.

Yet nothing but a favourable judgment from
the civilians in England could ultimately relieve
the mind of the adoring husband ; for while one
doubt remained in it, that he might yet bring affliction on his Emily, the dear delight of living
with her was imperfect pleasure.   Their return
home was once again in contemplation, when a
new cause of delay occurred, bringing with it the
sweetest hope in human nature.— Sir Edward was

suddenly struck with the same delicacy of complexion, that had fore-run the birth of his Emily, in herself; and by recalling the beloved remembrance of her mother, the Marchioness became doubly endeared to him. — How exquisite was the pleasure he gave to her husband in the hint! Both agreed that the timid Emily should choose her own time for disclosing a secret so pleasing to all three; and both with tender studious care promoted her every wish, nay sought in silence to anticipate them all.

Retirement was no longer thought necessary to the restoration of the Marchioness : but from the delicacy of her nature it now became her choice ; and she formed too entirely the happiness of her husband and father for them to wish to change the scene. — How indeed, when three informed and united hearts devoted every power to pleasing each other, could the enlargement of the party have improved it ?—Sir Edward among his studies pursued that of botany, and Emily delighted in drawing plants. — It became the favourite employment of her father and husband to discover in their rides and walks new subjects to amuse her mind, and engross her pencil. — She was engaged one evening in perpetuating a very perishable flower, while the Marquis was walking backwards and forwards in the saloon, trying upon his flute, from whence he drew most melting music, a thousand desultory strains, as they floated through his memory.—One struck Emily; but busied with her pencil, she hastily asked him, without raising her eye, where he had learnt that passage. — The Marquis paused, and, in the fluttered tone that to worldly observers would have announced insincerity, replied, that " he could not recollect;" though too well he remembered it was from Hypolito he learnt — it was with Hypolito he had often played it. — After a period of hesitation, the Marquis ventured in turn to inquire if she had ever heard it before.—" Certainly, my Lord," replied Emily, gaily smiling, and half raising her eyes — " it is a strain of my own; composed when I was a little rustic, wandering in the woods and wilds of Ireland, and thinking of my obstinate charming cousin : — it seemed something odd thus to hear the echo of my heart from your lips, especially as I never gave the air to more than one human being, and it was very improbable that she should ever fall in your way."

A strange cold tremor seized the frame of the
Marquis — Ah! God, thought he, who then was
that *one human being?* — Yet to discover even
the object of our fear is among the invariable,
though painful propensities of human nature. —
Almost breathless, he faltered out, at last, an inquiry. — The Marchioness replied, in the same
gay, careless tone, " I detest Ireland so thoroughly
from its having given you an unfavourable impression of your poor little wife, and Emily Fitzallen so much for having made my paternal mansion
a miserable home to me, that I never willingly
think of, much less mention, either one or the
other." — " And who," said the Marquis, in a
perturbed manner, " is this Emily Fitzallen ?"—
" Nay," cried his lady, " it is your own fault you
do not know ; for she has made no small figure
in my little history. I wonder my father never
told you the extraordinary scene we had, when
my grandmother's will was opened, with this upstart, insolent favourite. The proud, passionate
wretch, no sooner found herself thrown on my
mercy, — though well she knew she might have
trusted it, — than the fury glared at once through
the veil of her consummate beauty. I think even

now I see, and hear her, solemnly vowing a revenge on me, which happily it will never be in her power to execute; or hardly Heaven itself could save me;—so vindictive do I know her."

The Marquis, in an agony too mighty for expression, rushed out of the saloon, ere his groans should lead to the mysterious sorrow struggling at his heart, the yet happy daughter of Sir Edward. Thrown at his length in the garden, he tore his hair, and gave way to the frenzy of instantaneous, horrible conviction. " Oh ! Emily," exclaimed he, " adored, unfortunate Emily ! didst thou know how successful this fiend has already been, what but death could follow ? — Alas ! that is, perhaps, only for a little while delayed, and we shall both become her victims. The minute, inexplicable informations of that deliberate destroyer, that smiling Hypolito, are now accounted for : too well do I perceive the fiend yet walks this earth, vanishing at intervals, only to seduce me into such exquisite guilt, as shall give her, when she again appears, a yet more exquisite power of tormenting. That I should, till the moment I fell into the snare, have been ignorant of the existence of this serpent — and that I should *now — now* first learn it !

Oh ! just, yet killing punishment ! — blind, arrogant, wilful, I would not obey the voice of duty
or of gratitude. Alas ! my heart's dear Emily,
had I sought thee, as any other man would have
been proud to do, in the mansion of thy ancestors ; had I shown thee but the common respect
due to Sir Edward Arden's daughter, this monster
of iniquity would have been known to me ; and,
never, never could she thus fatally have accomplished her vengeance.

From the moment of this accidental explanation, which made no impression upon the mind of
the Marchioness, peace and rest fled from her
unhappy husband. The sad sense of an indistinct
impending evil which no human care could guard
against, together with the painful consciousness
of error, poisoned the dear delight of calling
Emily his own, and wore him down to a skeleton.

> " He withers at his heart ; and looks as wan,
> As the pale spectre of a murder'd man :
> Not, mix'd in mirth, in youthful pleasure shares,
> But sighs when songs and instruments he hears.
> Uncomb'd his locks, and careless his attire,
> Unlike the trim of love or gay desire."

Yet impelled by restlessness, continually to add

to the knowledge that devoured his very being,
when the Marquis entered into conversation at all,
it was to win, indirectly, from either Sir Edward
or Emily, more minute informations and recitals
concerning this detested impostor. The strange
singularity of her excelling on the flute was at
once accounted for by his wife, who informed him
that it had been the peculiar instrument of the
master who taught both the ladies at Bellarney;
and the bolder genius of Miss Fitzallen, she added,
ever pursued what pleased her, without a thought
of the proper or improper. Thus had she been
accustomed, in playing, always to accompany
Emily Arden; and in every accomplishment kept
pace with her.

The more the Marquis ruminated on the fatal
rite, which was the perpetual subject of his
thoughts, the more he became convinced that,
though a sudden resolve on his part, it was not so
on that of the seducing Hypolito, nor had been
imperfectly solemnised. The witnessing priests,
no less than the one who married him, were all
men high in consideration; and too well he knew
that the impostor had secured documents of the
ceremony, which he now plainly perceived no

wealth could purchase, no agonies win her to give
up. Never did he lift his eyes to the still unsuspicious Marchioness, that they were not ready to
overflow upon the lovely wretch, who knew not
yet her own misfortune.

The wan cheeks, the wild looks of the hapless
lover, could not, however, be equally guarded
from the observation of Sir Edward Arden, who
saw but too plainly some deep-seated sorrow in
his soul, which it was his only employment to hide
from his Emily — the beloved of both. In hours
of kindness and confidence, when they were alone,
Sir Edward often sought to lead his nephew to a
disclosure of his grief; but the effort generally
produced vague transports, threatening either
despair or madness; and glad was the afflicted
parent to retreat again into ignorance, so that he
could soothe to peace pangs wholly unintelligible.

A love thus steeped in tears is, however, too
trying a sight for a father. Sir Edward, again
unable to endure a state of total retirement, hinted
to the young pair that it might be adviseable to
return to Naples. Emily readily consented, from
the idea that the melancholy which she perceived
yet lurking about the Marquis, and now, she

feared, infecting her father, might proceed from
the sacrifice both made of society for her sake.
At Naples she should, at least, feel that both were
independent; nor would it be necessary for her
to mix in its gay circles.

Ah! hapless Emily, couldst thou have known
the misery awaiting thee at Naples, to the extremity of the earth wouldst thou have flown to
avoid it!—A few days after her return, the
Marchioness was persuaded, by her husband and
father, to drive, in their company, on the Corso.
Before her was one equipage, which they all perceived to be English. The slow parade of its
motion made the servants of the Marquis pass it
abruptly; and curiosity, to see who of their own
country it contained, induced all the party to lean
forward. A lovely face did the same in the other
carriage; and with a power scarce inferior to the
fabled one of the Gorgon, transfixed, in a manner,
a trio, who, at that moment, had not a single
thought of Miss Fitzallen. It was herself—that
fair fiend, gay, triumphant, elegantly attired, and
sumptuously attended. Her face was too strongly
impressed on Sir Edward's memory to be mistaken; to his daughter it seemed familiar as her

own; to the Marquis it appeared a vision of guilt
and horror. Had either of his companions instantaneously turned towards him, words would
not have been wanting to tell the cause of all his
silent struggles, of all his embittered enjoyments:
— his heart died within him, thus to find his worst
fear verified.

Emily, suddenly recollecting that to the Marquis this fatal face was unknown, turned to
account to him for the astonishment which it had
excited in herself and her father. She beheld him
sunk lifeless and low in the carriage; and snatch-
ing his hand, found on it the chill of death. Miss
Fitzallen was no more remembered; the whole
world vanished from the eyes of the tender wife;
and prognosticating a second attack of the Marquis's fearful fever, she hastened home to call
medical assistance, and use every possible precaution. Happily the common methods for alle-
viating the diseases of the body are the only ones
that can mitigate the anguish of the mind. Loss
of blood, abstinence, and solitude, misery requires
no less than fever. The last of these prescriptions
gave this unfortunate husband the painful pri-
vilege of shutting his door on all the world —

even on his adored Emily. Once more alone, he
would have regulated his ideas; but thought was
chaos. He would perhaps have died, had he
not known that he must alike kill the wife he
adored. He could only rend his hair and groan,
till exhausted nature sunk to stupefaction.

To address with supplication the heart base
enough to lead him on to guilt, the Marquis saw,
would be a vain attempt; and only show the infamous Miss Fitzallen the extent of power she had
acquired. To threaten might lead her to assert
it. — Whence, too, came she? How had she
escaped the horrors of the earthquake? how acquired the splendor with which she was sur
rounded? and under what name and character
was she received in society? Where could he
acquire self-command and patience enough to
pursue these inquiries? Yet, if they should ultimately tend to break the tie so abhorred, and
render Emily happy, was it not his duty to sacrifice every inferior feeling to that great one?

Under this impression, the Marquis again resolved to dissemble what was passing in his heart;
and, by mixing with the gay nobles of the Neapolitan court, trace out the history of this striking

stranger. What was his astonishment, when he returned into that circle, to find that she was no stranger there ; — that, while he was vainly seeking her in the character of Hypolito, without any disguise, and in her own name, Miss Fitzallen h ad appeared in Naples, almost from the day he left it ; — that she was considered as a beautiful Irish heiress, enchanting in her manners, and careless in her conduct. A woman who dares affect this character has all the male sex at once on her side. Not an associate of the Marquis who did not profess himself of her train ; yet not one impeached a life, by all admitted to be very equivocal. To his other cruel chagrins, the Marquis now added that of knowing, that if she should dare to assert her marriage, and the laws sanctioned it, she would bring on him, in her own person, indelible infamy; since it was sufficiently obvious she could have no wealth which vice did not procure. Yet so well are disgraceful secrets usually kept, that it might be for ever out of his power to prove the guilt which he in a manner witnessed. — But was it for him to attempt proving guilt on any other human being ? Did he not crawl upon the earth, the abhorred of his own

M 4

soul, and endure existence but for the sake of that
angel whom his adoration alone had sullied?
Such was the beginning, such the end, of the
daily, nightly meditations, of the Marquis of
Lenox.

Time, however, crept on; and no change in
the situation of any party occurred. Emily Fitzallen, occupied apparently with herself, her lovers,
and her own plans, seemed not to mean any further
to annoy the Marquis. Sir Edward and his
daughter knew not that they were to fear, and
soon became used to see her. Could the miserable Lenox, therefore, have compounded with his
conscience, he might yet have called his own that
happiness, which love, friendship, and fortune, in
rare union, sometimes lavish on humanity. Oh!
most acute of miseries, to remember his hand
only could have poisoned the rich cup of felicity!

But it was not the fate of the Marquis long to
enjoy even the little interval of rest which doubt
now gave him. The Duke of Aberdeen had at
length sent over to his daughter-in-law the splendid
jewels promised on her marriage. They were the
first set in the manner, since become so fashion-
able, called transparent. Emily's natural delicacy

made her decline appearing at court, as her person now showed her situation; but these beautiful
diamonds became so much the subject of discourse, that the Queen sent to desire the Marchioness would entrust them to her jeweller, to
alter some of her ornaments by.   The jewels were
committed to his care, and the cause of their not
being worn by their owner thus became public.
As any trifle will amuse the great, the jeweller's
house was immediately the resort of every lady
who had, or thought she had, a right to either
jewels or fashion.   Nor was Miss Fitzallen wanting to her own consequence on the occasion.   What
was the state of the Marquis, when, an hour after
her visit there, this billet was put into his hands:
— " Hypolito is charmed with the jewels; in
three days' time they must be sent, or you abide
the consequence."   The incensed and haughty
soul of the Marquis would have abided any consequence, but for the peculiar, the interesting,
situation of his Emily.   The mere fact, without
the least aggravation, would be death to her: but
with the colourings which this malignant fiend
might give it, madness would, perhaps, fore-run
some tremendous catastrophe.   After the most

desperate struggles with himself — an anguish past all description — the wretched Lenox tried to unfold a fabricated tale to his beloved, and saw, in the alarm that instantly shook her, what the truth would infallibly have produced in so delicate a creature. How sweet was the relief that glowed on her countenance, when she at last wrung from his labouring heart the fallacious confession, that he had incurred a debt of honour, beyond the utmost amount of the money at his immediate command, nor could payment be delayed. " The jewels alone" — Emily suffered him not to conclude the sentence : — " Take them at once, my love; take any, or all my fortune — Oh ! that the whole of it could restore colour to those bloodless cheeks, or peace to that beloved bosom ! well, indeed, then would it be employed : —

> ' For never should'st thou lie by Portia's side
> With an unquiet soul.' "

Who would not have endured a daily martyrdom for such a creature ? — Miss Fitzallen had the jewels she demanded. The only one the gentler Emily wished for, the heart of the Marquis, was wholly her own.

It happened, a short time after, that an English nobleman gave a *fête* ere he quitted Naples, to which of course the Marquis, his lady, and Sir Edward, were invited.   The Marquis shared not in any pleasure his Emily retired from; and she no longer mixed in company. Sir Edward, either from thinking the absence of the whole family would be an affront to their countryman, or a latent taste for gaieties he was not yet too far advanced in life to enjoy, accepted the invitation, though he joined not the party till late.   Among the masqued dancers, he suddenly perceived one who appeared to him to be adorned with the unworn jewels of the Marchioness.   Yet this was so unlikely, that her father drew near — rather to satisfy himself that they were not the same, than from the belief that they were.   It was not however possible to doubt their identity.   Neither would the wearer allow hers to be doubted; for when Sir Edward approached, Miss Fitzallen took off her masque, and, holding it carelessly in her hand, surveyed the incensed father with an exulting malignant smile, as though she bade him drink to the dregs the deadly poison of conviction.

Almost frantic with wrath and indignation, Sir

Edward rushed from the ball-room, and in one
moment would have rendered the two beings most
dear to him miserable for ever ; but that their
better angel bade them retire early, and escape the
storm.

Though the fever of passion raged all night in
Sir Edward's bosom, reason at intervals en-
deavoured to counteract it. In England, he recollected, that it was not unusual for arrogant
people to hire, at an extravagant price, additions
to their own diamonds, on occasions of parade.
The same custom might prevail at Naples; and
the queen's jeweller have availed himself of the
confidence reposed in him, to make a temporary
advantage of ornaments which he knew the owner
would not be near to recognise. This was possible, and only possible ; for Sir Edward hardly
could persuade himself that any jeweller would
venture to entrust diamonds so valuable at a masquerade, or that any person would choose to hire
a set so singular in their taste, as to prove they
could belong only to one lady. There was yet
another remote idea came to his relief (for it was
death to him to think but for a moment that
her husband had thus plundered and insulted his

daughter) —— Emily herself might have been acted
upon by this artful mean creature, and have given
her a princely fortune in her diamonds. He
remembered her having sent to Miss Fitzallen,
when she so insolently quitted Bellarney, all the
jewels she then possessed (for the bounty had been
haughtily and ungratefully returned into his own
hands): Emily might not, in the fervour of her
feelings at this period, have either taken into view
the vast difference in the value of the benefaction,
nor the disgrace which must result either to herself or her lord, in allowing a woman of a character at the best dubious, publicly to appear in
ornaments prepared for, and only suitable to, a
Duchess.

Morning, however, at length came ; and though
prudence had imposed present silence on Sir Edward, he was not the less determined to trace to
its source this extraordinary incident. When an
hour of loneliness gave him opportunity to examine how far his daughter was concerned, he
turned, as if accidentally, their conversation on
the jewels. Emily blushed, sighed, and strove, by
beginning on another subject, to wave that. Though
this effort too plainly proved that her diamonds

were gone, yet, in the painful state of the father's
mind, he was obliged rather to wish the egregious
folly of giving them away might be proved upon
his daughter, than a cruel doubt remain that her
husband had been guilty of ingratitude and baseness.   Sir Edward was on the point of reproving
Emily for thus unworthily bestowing the magnificent present of the Duke of Aberdeen, when his
native pride prevailed ; and, by his not deigning to
utter the name of Miss Fitzallen, his alarmed
daughter understood all he applied to that base
woman as referring to the Marquis : for it never
occurred to her, that she could be suspected, by
a human being, of having given to any creature
but her husband such valuables.   In her per-
plexity she betrayed, without designing it, how
she had disposed of them ; but, shocked at the
change in Sir Edward's face, extorted a promise of
secrecy from him, by the offer of unreserved confidence.   That promise was so necessary to his
learning the whole she could tell him, that he did
not hesitate to comply.   She then imparted the
specious tale of the Marquis's loss at the gaming-
table, and expressed the sweet relief her heart
found in taking from his the disgraceful weight of

a debt of honour. To smooth the furrows on her father's brow, Emily ventured to vouch for this debt being single in its kind, and generously called upon Sir Edward to rejoice that the first went to such an extent as would, in a rational mind, prevent a folly from becoming a habit. Sir Edward, though perhaps not more satisfied than at the beginning of the explanation, saw such merit and tenderness in Emily's conduct, that he yielded to her entreaties, and promised never to mention either the jewels, or the debt of honour, to the Marquis. On his own part he carefully supprest the painful knowledge which he had thus accidentally acquired; resolving, by future watchfulness, to fathom the heart of his nephew if the fault lay so deep, and to admonish him, if it should only influence his conduct.

Time, however, past on; and the married lovers, inseparable in their pleasures, gave no cause to the most watchful parent for dissatisfaction. Sir Edward had almost forgotten his cause of distrust; when, in a moment of hilarity, it not only was revived, but indelibly impressed. During a meeting of the dissolute Neapolitan nobles, with the gay travellers who wander from England to disseminate

the bad habits of their own country, and bring
home those of all they visit, Sir Edward found
Miss Fitzallen suddenly became the subject of
very light discourse, which began with her being
toasted by an Italian after the Marchioness, and
rejected by an Englishman as an improper asso-
ciation.   The sprightly sallies of gallantry and
admiration which this creature excited in her de-
fenders, would have been ill borne by Sir Edward,
had he not taken a strong interest in the subject,
from the desire he still had to learn the means by
which she obtained his Emily's jewels.   He now
began artfully to unbend; and the company with
eagerness listened to authority so indubitable,
when Sir Edward recounted all he knew of her
history: it concluded with his obvious desire to
benefit in turn by their communications, and a
marked wonder at the high style of her establishment, when he knew her to be without any inherited resources.   A laugh, that proved he had
shown ignorance where he might have been supposed to possess information, embarrassed Sir Edward, who, struggling to conceal his anxiety,
redoubled his address fully to develope the truth
which he almost trembled to know.   Without

hesitation, the thoughtless party spoke of a variety
of lovers as favoured by Miss Fitzallen, and lavish-
ing their wealth on her: but the most profuse,
they all admitted, was Count Montalvo, who
first took her from the Marquis of Lenox. Sir Edward Arden supposed his senses failed him; or
rather, that apprehension shaped into words the
workings of his fancy. The conversation, however, was gaily continued. Those who named the
Marquis, rather treated him as one who had formerly followed, than who now paid her homage.
Sick, sick at heart, the fond father smiled; though
on his lips the smile stiffened almost into a convulsion, that still he might hear: and hear he did.
The name of Hypolito at length was repeated;
and the start Sir Edward gave, showed this, as
applied to Miss Fitzallen, to be a discovery. He
was obliged to endure their raillery on his own
blindness, and be told, that almost every one
around him had discovered this favoured youth
to be a woman, who had thus disguised herself
to deceive the uncle, and make the nephew
happy.

And now, to the jaundiced sight of Sir Edward,
the whole horrible truth stood revealed in its most

odious colours.   In this nephew, so beloved, admired, esteemed, he suddenly beheld a man capable
of licentiousness and hypocrisy in the first instance
— baseness and ingratitude in the last.   He now
could recollect, that the features of this feigned
Hypolito had from the first struck him as familiar
to his eye : yet still they caused no suspicion ;
confiding, as he did at that time, in the Marquis,
and almost inseparable from both.   Having always seen in the impostor the talents, mien, and
manners, of a youth, how was it possible that he
should surmise her sex?   Yet well he remembered,
long after the earthquake at Messina, the agony of
the Marquis whenever Hypolito was named; and
he bitterly reproached himself for not reflecting,
that the feeling of man for man rarely produced so
pungent a pang.

     That the Marquis, at Messina, either by the
calamitous devastation or her own choice, had lost
the worthless wanton, was, to the erroneous judgment of Sir Edward, very evident : that he never
bestowed a thought on Emily Arden till that
moment seemed equally obvious.   It is true, when
they met, he condescended not to hate the gentle
creature who lived in his looks : nay, he even

deigned to marry her. But no sooner did the beautiful impostor appear, in the new charm of her own shape, than she resumed her full empire over the ungenerous Marquis; and he not only sacrificed to her his fortune and his honour, but feeling, nay even decency. " And such, then, is the husband whom I have a thousand times implored of Heaven for my innocent, my noble-minded Emily !" groaned forth the afflicted father.

One only hope of happiness remained to them all, in the judgment of Sir Edward, and that was a hope horrible to humanity. A single lover might not be able to attach Miss Fitzallen; a single fortune certainly could not support her: and if once the Marquis discovered the first, her reign would be over. Sir Edward had bound himself to endure the scene before him with patience, and he determined he would do so; although his secret soul misgave him, that the fair fiend, if she ruined not the husband by her extravagance, would sooner or later destroy the wife by her malice.

The favourite and trusted valet of Sir Edward knew his master too well not to comprehend something of the unspoken cares that preyed on his peace. From that domestic, Sir Edward had the

additional vexation of learning, that every servant
in the family had, from the first, suspected the sex
of the feigned Hypolito; and all concluded that it
was a love affair of the young Lord's, which his
uncle would not see.   He, too, confirmed the
opinion of his master, that, in the earthquake at
Messina, this disguised favourite vanished : and
the affliction her lover long showed, proved he believed her among the victims.

By means of his valet, in whom he was reduced
to confide, Sir Edward had a strict watch kept on
the wanderings of the melancholy Lenox; but,
from these, malice could not have drawn any conclusion against him.   No being could point out
the moment which he passed not in lonely misery,
save those he beguiled in the society of Emily and
her father.   Yet the latter now sought him not,
still less condescended, to sooth him.   Each had
his own oppressive secret to guard; and the Marchioness became soon the only link between two
hearts, that once preferred each other to the whole
world.

Nor was even Emily without a latent fear, —a
buried sorrow. Among her insipid Italian female visitants, one had been found capable of shocking her

with the information of the name of the lady who now possessed and displayed the rich baubles that seemed to have been sent only to torment her : and though it was possible that the winner of the immense debt, which those jewels were appropriated to pay, had gratified Miss Fitzallen with them, it was likewise possible that the Marquis himself might have been the donor. The long absences, which he rendered every day longer, perplexed and afflicted his wife; who, more and more confined from her situation, had ample leisure for conjecture. Had she too set a spy on the Marquis, well would she have known, that the periods when he no longer gladdened her sight were always spent by him in the deepest shade of some convent garden, in solitude, penitence, groans, and anguish.

The days that now passed rapidly to the fearful Emily seemed to creep to the Marquis, who expected, with more than a lover's impatience, with more than a father's anxiety, the one which would render her a mother : when her recovery would leave him at liberty to hasten to England, and satisfy his mind as to the predicament in which the laws of that country placed him. By those of

Italy, he knew himself condemned, unless Miss
Fitzallen consented to prove the marriage incomplete.   It was a situation too delicate to intrust to
any human being; nor dared he on paper commit
himself.   Every day, every hour, he repeated with
what impatience he should hasten, when able, to
England; and even Sir Edward, not knowing
how to reconcile this lively anxiety to return, with
the charm he still fancied Italy contained for the
Marquis, now gave him credit for reviving virtue,
and now despised him for consummate hypocrisy.
    Sir Edward foreseeing how little Emily would
like to mix in the Neapolitan society, and quite
convinced that it was necessary, in her condition,
to take exercise and amusement, had for some
time meditated surprising her with a useful present.
He had, therefore, ere she left the country, employed his grooms to break a set of beautiful
Spanish horses; and sent for a light, low, elegant
kind of carriage, which ladies often safely drive.
The rides round Naples are beautiful, but not
contiguous; and thus was the Marchioness to be
seduced into exploring them.   The sweetly fancied
carriage, however, was no sooner seen, than like
her diamonds, it became the object of universal

attraction.   Miss Fitzallen was among those whom
it captivated ; — to admire, and to appropriate,
was, with her, the same thing.   The success of
her first bold demand ensured her whatever
she required of the Marquis ; and another peremptory billet from her almost overset his
reason.   The little equipage in question had not
been *his* gift; it had no comparative value; nor.
could human ingenuity invent a mode of obtaining
it from the generous owner that would not wound
her to the heart.   Yet, too certainly, the fiend
must be silenced.   A day and night of exquisite
torture, on the part of the Marquis, announced to
Emily some other impending affliction ; when her
tenderness wrung from his sad soul an insincere
confession, that he had, in an hour of accidental
inebriation, wantonly staked her little favourite
carriage and horses ; which having lost, he found,
to his unspeakable chagrin, no equivalent would be
accepted, nor any thing on earth but the simple
stake.   The tender Emily listened, but it was no
longer with an implicit reliance on his honour and
veracity.   Neither could she find, in this recital,
however agitated his manner, that openness or
probability, by which his actions had been here-

tofore characterised.   Yet it was certain, whatever
the cause, that he greatly desired the beautiful
trifle in question ; and it was still her duty, as it
had always been her delight, to comply with every
wish of his.   She faintly hinted a fear of offending
her father ; but bade the Marquis honourably acquit himself to his inexorable opponent : nor could
she account for the burning drops, which her cheek
the next moment imbibed from that of her husband, as with a long embrace he strained the generous charmer to his heart.

Perhaps rather to please her father than herself, Emily had shown a singular delight in this
little carriage ; and he had fully felt the delicacy
of her gratitude.   She now continually made
excuses for staying at home, which Sir Edward
sought to overrule ; and, after a time, confessed
her health to be his motive.   His daughter became chagrined and embarrassed.   A secret consciousness that she had not wholly relied upon
the account of the Marquis, as to the disposal of
her father's present, made her hesitate to own she
had parted with it.   She, therefore, slightly answered, that the Spanish horses were too spirited.
Sir Edward was leaving her to talk to the grooms

on that subject, when his daughter, with increasing
embarrassment, added, that the alarm she had
taken had made her resolve to put it out of her
own power to risk so dangerous an indulgence in
future, by desiring the Marquis to change the
carriage with one of his friends, who was urgent
to get such another. The simplicity of this
account, though he might have thought his little
gift too slightly valued, would, at another time,
have entirely satisfied Sir Edward ; but, watchful
as he was now become, and sweetly ingenuous as
Emily had ever been, it was impossible but he
must perceive that she veiled the fact, if she was
too upright to falsify it.

To accord with her father's wish, as far as was
in her power, the Marchioness then ordered her
coach to be made ready : and, attended by her
woman, drove to the Corso. What a spectacle
awaited her there ! Miss Fitzallen, in all the insolence of exultation, seated in the beautiful carriage, so lately Emily's, was driving the same
horses in the English style, to the admiration of
a set of Italian nobles, by whom she was surrounded. Hardly could Sir Edward's gentle
daughter suppose even her vindictive nature ca-

pable of an outrage so gross : but her woman then
in attendance could not forbear confirming the
fact, by an exclamation of disdain. At that moment, the gay, insulting fiend, perceiving by the
livery who was approaching, made her coursers
fly as close as she dared to the coach of the
Marchioness; who, lifting her tearful eyes to
Heaven, pressed her hands in silence upon the
heart that had betrayed her peace, in adoring, as
she believed, a worthless object, and sunk back
in a swoon.

The proud career of Miss Fitzallen was, however, something checked, by her meeting, in the
way to her hotel, Sir Edward Arden. His indignant eye suddenly fell from herself to the well-
known horses : again it was pointedly raised to
her face, and again, with contempt and fury,
glanced upon the carriage. A look informed
him, that the base woman who had, through the
Marquis, thus poorly plundered his daughter, had
not the decency to expunge from her acquisition
even the arms of Lenox. Sir Edward stopped
his horse a moment, as dizzy and stupified; but
recovering himself, turned the animal round, and
was presently by the side of Miss Fitzallen, who

felt not quite easy at finding he meant to accompany her. She slackened the reins, and summoned all her resolution, when she saw him alight at the same moment she did, and abruptly follow her into her own hotel. Passing into the first apartment, from a something of fear which, dauntless as was her character, she could not control, she threw herself into a seat; and, with her usual insolent air, demanded to know to what extraordinary occasion she was to impute the intrusion of Sir Edward Arden. "The intrusion is so extraordinary to himself," returned that gentleman, "when he considers the company he has joined, that he will speak to the point, and spare discussion : — all other feelings are lost in those of the father. I come not, Madam, to *ask* aught. I come to *command* you to efface, from the beautiful bauble which you have just quitted, the arms of the Marquis of Lenox. Though he may empower you to destroy the peace of his wife, it remains with her father to guard her honour." — " Have a care, Sir Edward," returned the lady, suffering all the fury to glare over her fine features, — " have a care how you venture any *command* to me. If ever your daughter carries a

point in which I am concerned, it must be by very
different means." — "Weak, insolent, wanton
woman!" cried Sir Edward, with increasing bitterness, "do you mistake me for the worthless
young man, over whom you tyrannise with a
power so absolute? Do you think it possible that
I should ever level his mistress with his wife?" —
"Address to your own daughter," retorted the
lady with a smile of diabolical triumph, "those
gross terms, which are entirely misapplied when
lavished on me. *Command her* to efface from her
carriage the arms of the Marquis of Lenox. Bid
her lay down *my* title; and when you henceforth
speak of the mistress of your nephew, think of
Emily Arden; when you mention his wife, remember only *me*."

Too powerful was the emotion of Sir Edward's
nature at this assertion, incredible as the fact appeared, for him to utter a single syllable. Miss
Fitzallen, after a pause, resumed — "I can easily
guess how little weight my claim would have, did
it depend only on my own word, or your idolised
nephew's honour. But I have full, authentic documents, which prove me to have been the wife of
the Marquis, months before he, in idle pageant,

gave that name to your daughter. Here," cried she, opening a locket which hung at her bosom, and taking from it the witnessed certificate, which she spread before the miserable father's sight, — " is one irrefragable proof that our marriage was solemn, regular, and valid."

Sir Edward Arden's quick eye, rendered even more quick by disdain, saw (and seeing, recognised) the handwriting of Padre Anselmo, with whom he had once held a literary correspondence; nor were the names of the witnessing priests unknown to him. Wrought up as he was to the last extreme of suffering nature, the dignity of his mind did not desert him. With that lofty obeisance, which is rather a respect paid to ourselves than the object before us, Sir Edward in silence admitted the claim, however insolently made, and abruptly withdrew; while in his pallid countenance too visibly appeared the deep, the uncontrolable anguish of his soul.

Nor was it anguish alone the insulted father felt — unconquerable indignation, burning rage, strung every nerve, and the storm burst only with more dreadful violence for his having allowed it to collect with a deceiving stillness. Calmly mounting his horse, he rode home, and there giving it to his groom, retired as usual to his own apartment. Having taken thence a pair of pistols that he always kept in high order, and ready loaded, he resorted to a convent garden, which his spy had informed him was among the favourite haunts of the lonely, melancholy Marquis.

Sir Edward was too successful in his research. In the most retired spot of the sacred ground, where a deep shade extended over an oratory, thrown at his length on a stone seat near the entrance, and lost in mournful meditation, was the interesting object of Sir Edward's fury. There had been a time when thus to have seen his darling nephew would have melted Sir Edward to the weakness of childhood. The waste of the young man's graceful form was never more visible. His wild and hollow eyes now scanned heaven impatiently, and now sunk heavily to the ground. No sense of pleasure — no flow of youthful vigour — was now to be traced in the unhappy Lenox. Yet did not his countenance bespeak the perturbation of guilt. A silent, sullen, impenetrable sorrow lived there; which, hoping nothing, demanded nothing: but draining as it were the sap from the tree, left it without life, though it fell not.

Yet who can wonder, that, in the deep sense of present injury and outrage, Sir Edward Arden lost for a moment the acute sensibility, nay, even the humanity, of his nature? Fiercely approaching, without deigning a word, he offered to the unfortunate youth, who hastily started up on seeing his uncle, one of the pistols, and waved to him haughtily to take his ground. Desirable from any other hand would have been the death which the Marquis dared not give himself; but from his uncle! — the father of his Emily! He gazed on his lost friend in mute misery, intuitively aware how he had lost him; then, taking with the pistol, the hand that held it, in fond agony he kissed, he clasped it: it was the hand that had cherished his infancy — the hand that had given him the sad invaluable blessing, which, even now, he knew not how to part with. Sir Edward snatched his hand away with a fury that nearly threw his nephew backwards. " Coward too are you, as well as villain?" cried he, with almost inarticulate passion. " Double your infamous perjury — swear to me that you are not married to Miss Fitzallen —

that you did not deliberately dishonour" — his native pride would not allow him to finish the sentence. In a tone even yet more choked, he resumed, waving with his pistol the due distance to the Marquis, " Take your ground, sir; keep your guard; worthless as you are, I would not be your murderer."

The youth had arisen, and a faint flush, at the personal insult of his uncle, gave a wild indignant charm to his natural beauty : but he spoke not — moved not — nor, though he held the pistol, did he lift it. Sir Edward observed him no more; but, conforming to the modes of duels, retreated properly, and turning, impetuously fired — alas ! with but too sure an aim. In one moment he beheld his nephew in the agonies of death. Passion expired — human resentment and injury were at once forgotten — and he who had killed the wretched young man hung lamenting over him, even like a fond father whom some unforeseen stroke had rendered childless. The Marquis perhaps accelerated his own fate, by a fruitless effort which he again made to seize and kiss his uncle's hand. After a dreadful struggle, he at length found voice to cry, "Fly, save yourself.— Oh God!

pity, preserve my Emily; leave me *to*"—life now flitted from him, and Sir Edward remained a monument of horror.

And it is thus we daily arrogate to ourselves the bloody right of adding crime to crime, and call it honour — justice! an impious law, by which proud man lives to himself alone, and defies his Maker!

In the Neapolitan government, as well as many other Italian ones, justice is lame as well as blind; and he must be a lagging criminal, indeed, who cannot escape so tardy a pursuer. Hot and impetuous spirits have, therefore, often presumed to right themselves, and personal vengeance has become an almost licensed evil in civil society. The safety of Sir Edward was not endangered, he well knew, by a duel; but the spot on which it had taken place was hallowed: nor could he, being a protestant, claim sanctuary with the monks, therefore he knew himself liable to be seized for sacrilege. In the situation of Emily this would be consummate ruin; and for her sake only did he think it necessary to guard against being stopt in retreating from the garden. Recollecting that the loaded pistol would enable him to command

his freedom; he approached again the body of
his nephew, taking it from his lifeless hand, near
which he dropt the fatal one he had himself fired.
What cruel pangs seized upon his heart as kneeling,
he fondly gazed upon the wan visage of the Marquis, and groaned forth the name of his sister!
Each feature seemed moulded by death to a yet
stricter resemblance of those long buried in the
grave. — Again Sir Edward returned; again he
wept; again he smote his breast; and willingly
would he have laid down his own life, to restore
that he had so rashly taken.

It happened the part of the convent-ground upon
which the Marquis had fallen was at certain hours
open to all visitants; nor did Sir Edward, either
at entering or retiring, meet a single being. Not
daring to risk one look from his widowed daughter,
he retreated to an hotel, and summoned his valet,
a rational man in middle life, on whose conduct
and fidelity he could fully rely. Having hastily
and imperfectly imparted to this trusty domestic
the fatal fact, he bade him think, if possible, how
it could be for a time concealed from the unfortunate Emily; and how she might be wrought
upon to remove from the terrible scene of her

husband's death, before she knew she had lost him.

Sir Edward's valet, who had long seen some heavy evil brooding in the three bosoms, was less surprised than shocked at the present one. After pausing a moment, he recalled to Sir Edward's recollection, that in the bay lay prepared, by the orders of the Marquis, for a little voyage to the neighbouring isles, a small pleasure bark, which that nobleman had purchased. This might in a few hours be ready to put to sea, and would be, in fact, the only way a lady in the condition of the Marchioness could venture to travel, as well as a secure mode of avoiding either following couriers, or accidental intelligence. He proposed imme-diately hastening to her, that by a partial com-munication of the truth, he might prevent her from a more close inquiry. The Marchioness would easily, he thought, be persuaded to embark, if assured that both her husband and father had been engaged in a duel, in consequence of which, though unwounded, they were obliged to fly. In the interim, he promised to keep so strict a guard at home, that no alarm should reach her ear, till she was again in her father's protection: but, not so easy for his master's safety as Sir Edward himself was, he exhorted him to mount his horse; and, posting through the Neapolitan dominions, make the utmost speed to gain those of the Pope.

The distracted state of Sir Edward's mind caused him at once to acquiesce in those minute arrangements which he had hardly power to comprehend, much less make. His horses were soon ready; and, as motion seems always a temporary relief to an overcharged soul, he involuntarily complied with the advice of his faithful domestic, in hastening towards Rome, which he reached without attracting any observation.

The faithful valet of Sir Edward felt all the weight of the charge and disclosure which he had undertaken, when he learnt that the Marchioness had been brought home from the Corso in fits, and was now shut up in her chamber. From her woman, however, he heard not any thing that implied a knowledge of the truth; and, having despatched orders to the mariners to prepare to sail in two hours, he imparted to the domestics Sir Edward's directions to get immediately together whatever might be necessary for their lady's accommodation, when she should be ready to go on board. While this was doing, he underwent the most painful apprehension, lest the body of the unfortunate Marquis should be brought home for interment, with the rude train of an unfeeling mob. The hours, however, passed on, and nothing alarming occurred. From the abrupt and broken manner in which Sir Edward had spoken of the rencounter, the place where it happened had never been mentioned; nor dared the prudent valet risk any inquiry, or venture out of the house, lest he should show prior information.

The bark was now ready; and the servants having made due preparations, Sir Edward's valet desired to be admitted to Emily, whom he found lying on the bed, weak, dejected, and tearful: but she in a moment sprang impatiently from it, on being told that her husband and father were obliged to fly, and implored her to hasten after them. The sad circumstances she was in, so much to others the object of consideration as to detain the whole family for months at Naples, vanished at once from the mind of the impassioned wife — the affectionate daughter. Could an unborn child engross a thought, when the life of the father was in question?

The bark of the Marquis was only one of many which the nobles of Naples keep in the bay for parties of pleasure; and those who saw Emily carried cheerfully into it annexed no idea to her departure but that of amusement: and indeed the season was so favourable, and the shore so lovely, as to render this a very natural conclusion.

The widowed, interesting Emily, as yet unconscious of her own misfortune, was no sooner off the shore of Naples, than a sudden lightness seized her heart. Its tormentor was left behind; and surely would not venture to pursue the Marquis, to whom she fondly supposed herself hastening. The duel she immediately concluded to have been between the Count Montalvo and her husband; the former being generally spoken of as the favoured lover of Miss Fitzallen, and the latter but too probably as his rival. She anxiously questioned the valet of Sir Edward: but he, who in reality was informed of very little, would not repeat that little, and only insisted, that he knew Sir Edward and the Marquis had been together.

Ah! if they were indeed so, and in harmony with each other, might not this rencounter have the happiest consequences, in removing from the eyes of the Marquis that film which an illicit love had spread over them?   With what facility does the heart adopt every idea that favours its feelings ! The fancy of Emily now sweetly pictured her husband returning to her in confidence and love. She saw his amiable penitence — she heard his vows of future unalienable faith — she enjoyed the fond delight which she should find in forgiving his errors, the endeared charm she might obtain in his eyes, by forgetting them.   The most balmy slumbers followed contemplations so innocent and affectionate; and, when the Marchioness awaked in the morning, she found herself in better health and spirits than she had known for a long time.

The little voyage was, by the management of Sir Edward's valet, ingeniously prolonged, though Emily knew it not, that his master might have time to prepare for her reception at Frescati, where Sir Edward had some months before procured a villa, as an occasional residence for himself, to which it had been settled his hapless daughter should be conveyed.   When the agreed time had elapsed, the bark put in at Civita Vecchia, where a litter, with some domestics of Sir Edward's, was

found to be in waiting.   The interesting Marchioness, supported by the energies of mind against
the weakness of sex and situation, lost not a moment in rest at the port, but hastened to Frescati ;
impelled by a generous hope which she was not
permitted to realise, that she should speak peace and
consolation to one, or both, of those waiting there
for her arrival.

Like a worn wretch, who had never known
quiet or rest since she saw him last, stood at the
gate to receive her Sir Edward Arden: but, dear
as he was, her heart demanding one yet dearer,
she cast her eyes anxiously round the saloon, into
which her father led her, in impatient silence. The
swell of pride, which grief had a little allayed in
her absence, burst out in all its violence, when
Sir Edward cast his eyes on his dishonoured child,
ready to bring into the world a memento of perpetuated ignominy.   So powerful was the impression, that all other considerations vanished from his
mind ; and, when Emily, in faltering accents, en-
quired for her husband, the indiscreet indignant
father clasped her in his arms, and, in a haughty
tone, exclaimed — " Unhappy girl, you have no
husband; you never had one; the wretch who,

under that name, dishonoured you, or is already married to Miss Fitzallen : but he has expiated his crimes against us both with his life." Emily, who had made a violent effort to sustain herself, lest the truth should not be allowed to reach her ear, at these words, with almost supernatural strength, sprang from her father's arms, and, turning on him a look of mute repulsive horror, staggered to a couch, where throwing herself on her face, she shut out with recollection for a time, the deep sense of incurable anguish, — utter despair.

Sir Edward, sensible too late that he had risked, by this abrupt avowal, incurring a second misfortune, not inferior in magnitude to the one he was lamenting, summoned her women to Emily, and warned them to be tender and careful of her. Long, long was it ere they could recal her to life— Ah ! what was life to Emily?

> " Why should she strive to catch convulsive breath,
> Why know the pang, and not the peace of death ?"

Existence was perhaps only prolonged in her, by the agonizing effort which nature obliged her to make to bestow it. After a few hours of acute suffering, the nurses put into the arms of the

exhaust~ ~ ~dowed mother, a poor little girl. —
By ~ ~ ~ fine working of the human soul is it,
that we sometimes extract raptures from agony,
and sweetness from shame? The first cry of the
child was a claim on the mother's affections,
which time could never weaken; and, under all
the sad circumstances attending the infant's birth,
Emily was proud to fold to her bosom a daughter
of the Marquis of Lenox.

Far otherwise were the feelings of Sir Edward;
nature made him wish to preserve his daughter;
but in his wounded heart lived a faint hope that
the offspring of so many sorrows would not survive to prove only a grievous record of them.
The joy which the arrival, and promise of continued life in the little stranger, gave to his domestics, shocked and offended him; nor did he
less offend or shock all the females of his family,
by peremptorily refusing to see the infant, and
forbidding them to speak of it, unless an inquiry
came from him.

Torn as Sir Edward was by grief and remorse,
his pride still prompted him to guard against the
persecuting fiend, whose machinations, any more
than her rights, might not end with the life of

the Marquis. But the passions of powerful minds take so high a tone from the understanding, that it is not easy for common observers to discriminate between their faults and their virtues. Actuated by that dignified pride, which, daring to humble itself to the dust, leaves the mean, or malignant, without any power of humbling it at all, Sir Edward Arden immediately resolved that his daughter should not appropriate aught that any human being had a right to take from her. Calling, therefore, together her domestics, and his own, he ordered the former to throw off the liveries of the Marquis of Lenox, and expunge his arms from her carriages; concluding with a stern command to the astonished circle, never more to mention the name of his nephew in his hearing, or to call his daughter by any other than that which he himself bore. His tone showed he would be obeyed; and he was so by all the family, but Emily's own woman, Mrs. Connor.

This grievous effort being made to provide against the future attacks of the infamous Miss Fitzallen, Sir Edward resolved never again, if possible, to see, certainly never more to exchange a syllable with her, whatever steps either to sooth or exasperate him, or his daughter, she might hereafter take.

The morose humour in which Sir Edward had long been, with the solitary life he now affected, co-operated with this singular and severe command, to give the servants an idea that his senses were touched by the death of the Marquis; which the daily, nightly lamentations of the miserable Emily at once published in the family. It was whispered, universally, that the unfortunate youth had ended his own days; which, though it occasioned much sorrow among the domestics, gave them little surprise. In fact, they had long apprehended that his wasting health and mysterious melancholy would have that horrible termination.

This idea soon became no less general at Rome; and Sir Edward found, to his own astonishment, that the tremendous secret of who had ended the life of the Marquis was confined to his own breast, and that of the valet, to whom he had himself confided it.

Cardinal Albertini, a prelate of the first rank and merit at Rome, who had long been in habits of particular friendship with Sir Edward, and who much admired and esteemed the Marquis, now, with sympathetic tenderness, conveyed to the former a regular account of the melancholy fate of his nephew, as transmitted to the holy college by the superior of the convent where the body had been found. It expressed, without any doubt, that the unknown young man must have been his own executioner, as only one pistol had been found lying by him; and two balls, which were lodged in his side, had been indisputably discharged from that pistol.

Sir Edward on reading this awful memorial, recollected with mute horror, having taken from the lifeless hand of his nephew the loaded pistol; though, in so doing, he only sought to secure his own departure from the convent, nor deigned to meditate veiling his guilt.

He resumed the letter. The fathers of the convent were unacquainted with the English tongue; and all the letters and papers found on the body were unfortunately in that language. The disgrace of having had their holy precincts stained with blood, made them so cautious who they called in as a translator, that some time elapsed before they could be sure the miserable victim of his own rashness was identically the

Marquis of Lenox.   A faithful brother was then
despatched in search of his worthy uncle, Sir
Edward Arden; but, through a singular and unlucky chance, he was just gone by sea, with his
daughter, on a party of pleasure to Frescati.
The melancholy duty of interment admitting, as
must be obvious, of no delay, the Marquis had
been buried with the utmost privacy, and the
whole transaction as yet kept a secret in Naples.
It was now submitted to the Holy Father of the
church to judge of their proceedings; and give
such instructions for informing the young nobleman's relations as he, in his piety and wisdom,
should see fit.

So extraordinary a circumstance as that of
having, by mere accident, escaped the odious
stigma attending a duel with his nephew, was
matter of perpetual astonishment to Sir Edward.   But it is not in the secrecy of its fault
that a noble mind finds any mitigation of suffering:
the specious palliations, the extenuating pleas,
which self-love boldly urges against the censures of
the world, an ingenuous nature dares not bring
before the secret tribunal of conscience, where
man sits sole judge of his own actions on this side

of the grave. At that tribunal, Sir Edward Arden every day, every hour, pronounced his own condemnation; and the image of his bleeding, dying nephew, fondly striving to clasp the unrelenting hand which had struck at his life, was for ever present to his eyes.

How is it that our deep sense of a past fault prevents not the commission of a new one? Had compunction operated to amendment, Sir Edward would, with endeared fondness, have soothed the daughter whom he had widowed, and have kept in his "heart of hearts" the babe he had rendered fatherless. But his nature was unequal to sorrowing for more than one object; and, while he lamented the dead, he shunned, nay almost hated, the innocent causes of his crime.

That Emily should shrink from her father's sight was, in her weak and melancholy situation, too natural. The little sensibility he had shown for her, in abruptly disclosing her loss, with its mortifying and calamitous occasion, was never absent from her mind. The harsh and cruel sound of his voice, when pronouncing *"you have no husband — you never had one,"* — rang like the knell of death for ever in her ears; nor did her ignorant attendant, Mrs. Connor, leave her unacquainted with the humiliating command Sir Edward had given, that she should be called in in future Miss Arden only: thus marking with opprobrium the precious infant that once was to inherit the highest hopes, — superior rank, — immense fortunes. When life had thus lost every charm to the widowed Emily, the recollection that in the grave she should elapse from the authority of this severe father, — that the killing tone of his voice could there no more wither her heart, — that she should, at last, sleep in peace with the Marquis of Lenox, — made that cold retreat, human nature commonly shrinks from, to her a dear and desirable asylum. To the poor infant, when the nurses put it into her arms, Emily would mournfully whisper, — " *Thou*, my beloved innocent, wilt grow up, as thy mother never did, under that severe eye, which will, perhaps, deign to beam tenderness on thee, when she can offend no more. *Thou* wilt not shudder at the sound of that decisive voice; for the destruction of thy happiness it may never announce: *thou* art among the few, the very few, to whom the loss of parents may be ultimately a blessing."

Feelings and lamentations like these might well, in the reduced state of Sir Edward's daughter, urge on the fate she implored.　A slow fever seized her, and having first robbed the babe of its natural nourishment ; finally left the mother hardly power to receive any to recruit her strength.　Dr. Dalton began to be alarmed, and apprised Sir Edward of the precarious state in which he thought the lady.　Her father started, as from a dream, and almost envied the fate Emily was threatened with.　Her danger increased; and as Sir Edward was one day gloomily ruminating on its probable termination, he suddenly recollected, that in the singular predicament in which his daughter was placed, by this disputable marriage, her child's right to the immense inheritance vested in herself might one day be contested, perhaps with success, by the remote heirs of the Bellarney family ; unless, as Emily was now turned of twenty-one, she made a will, clear and unequivocal, in favour of her daughter.　To suggest so mortifying as well as alarming a measure, to a young creature on the verge of the grave, required all the firmness of Sir Edward : but he calculated his own feelings at so high a rate, as to fancy he imposed upon

himself, in seeing the mother and a child he abhorred, while he discussed this odious and painful
necessity, a suffering quite equal to that of Emily.

If to see his daughter was an effort to Sir Edward, the receiving his visit was almost death
to Emily: she no sooner heard the sound of his
feet at the chamber door, than she shrunk into the
arms of her attendants, and fell into fainting fits.
The horrible remembrance of his last abrupt disclosure made, however, all he could now say more
trying in the apprehension than reality. It might
be too true, that the unhappy child, were her
legitimacy undisputed, could not inherit the en-
tailed estates of the Lenox family, and Sir Edward
himself had but a competence to give. The fortune of Emily alone could be rendered its ample
provision; and to prevent future law-suits with
her heirs on the maternal side, she must, Sir Edward insisted, by will secure all her property to
the infant.

The tender mother, and obedient daughter, gave
no other reply to her father's discourse, than that
she submitted to his judgment the right and proper,
and should fulfil this last duty to him and to her
child, whenever he called upon her.

But what a trying duty did it prove to the poor Emily, when the moment came for her to hear read, in the presence of the necessary witnesses, this legal instrument. Conscious, through the whole term of her existence, only of generous tenderness, of hallowed obedience, of every pure and virtuous feeling, that softens or elevates humanity, the innocent daughter of Sir Edward, the wife of the Marquis of Lenox, was obliged to hear herself ignominiously recorded as Emily Arden; and the fatherless babe at her bosom, not allowed to derive even a name from the noble family of her husband, alike termed Emily Arden, as the only mode of securing it from poverty. Nor was Sir Edward's proud and embittered spirit less overwhelmed; he seemed almost frantic.

The sweet saint, who was the more immediate sufferer, with pale composure desired to be lifted and supported in her bed; and bending solemnly over her child, raised her hands awhile in earnest, though silent, supplication to Heaven; then meekly kissed and blessed the smiling cherub. — " Dear child of misfortune, memento of misery," sighed she, " become not its sad inheritor. Be the pangs of thy father, the anguish of thy mother, in the sight of God, sweet babe, a merit to thee ! and, through his mercy, whatever name the pride of man may give or take from thee, may'st thou ripen into a blessing to all who cherish thy little being, an honour to him who bestowed it !" — Emily then signed the memorable will ; and duly delivering it, inclined towards her kneeling father with touching dignity, as bending for his blessing; and finding it only in his sobs, turned away in silence, waving thence all the spectators ; as though her life had been closed by this act of Christian grace and sad submission.

That lively remembrance of the past, which made Sir Edward Arden's days a burden to him, recurred with additional force after this severe trial of his feelings. He found that he never could be any comfort to his unhappy daughter ; and felt she was a caustic to the wound ever bleeding in his heart. He therefore determined to withdraw awhile ; and by mixing in the lettered circles of Rome, to diversify his thoughts, which, in solitude, dwelt ever on a single object.

Among the grievous and odious necessities of Sir Edward's situation, had been that of giving information to the Duke of Aberdeen of his son's early and dreadful catastrophe. — Unwilling to avow the guilt which he was ashamed to conceal, he had forborne addressing the childless duke, till Cardinal Albertini sent to him the simple record of the Neapolitan monks. — A copy of this he could remit, without implicating himself; and in his own narration he only included the account of the Marquis's fixed attachment to Miss Fitzallen, and the gross insults that followed towards his wife; — the arrogant assertion made by that worthless woman of her legal rights, and his carrying his daughter from Naples in consequence of this discovery. — He concluded with describing the decided manner in which he had obliged his daughter to recede from a disgraceful contest, by laying down the title of the Marquis; and called upon the Duke to bewail with him the birth of a grand-child, who could only remain a grievous memento to both, of the crime of the father, and the misfortune of the mother.

It is ever in the power of virtuous and enlightened minds to pour balm into the deep wounds of human calamity. — Sir Edward Arden's friends at Rome well knew the heavy visitations in his own family, which had shaken his character, and preyed upon his peace: all, therefore, with unremitting kindness, assimilated themselves in his sorrows, till insensibly their severity abated. — The venerable Cardinal Albertini particularly sympathised with him, and hardly more for his own sake than his nephew's. The sweetness of temper, elegance of manners, and frankness of heart, that had ever characterised the Marquis of Lenox, caused him to leave an impression on the minds of those to whom he had been known, not common for young noblemen of his age to make, when on their travels. — It was therefore sensibility, and not curiosity, which actuated the cardinal, to learn, if possible, from Sir Edward the unknown cause of that deep despair, which had, in the young man, so fatal a termination, as that described by the Neapolitan monks' memorial.

There are moments when the surcharged heart cannot resist the secret workings of unmerited kindness. — In one of these the afflicted father disclosed all of the tale, but the sad truth that his own hand had shortened the days of his nephew. — He amplified on the joy he had taken in the birth of the Marquis — on the love he had ever borne him — described the mortal chagrin which his nephew's coldness towards the bride proposed to him, in his own daughter, had often given him;

and passing from thence to the history of Emily,
described her innocent predilection, her successful
little romance, and the peace all were in, when he,
and his nephew, quitted England. — Sir Edward
now came upon the imposture of Miss Fitzallen,
and the fatal success of the diabolical artifice. —
But it was not possible for him to trace the infamous means by which she had kept her hold on
the young man, inducing him to injure, as well as
insult, that amiable creature whose honour she
had at last sullied, by claiming the Marquis as
her husband, and whose days she would as certainly shorten in having caused so horrible a
catastrophe.

. Hardly could a stoic have heard a father tell
his own sad story thus impressively without
emotion : the venerable cardinal was all sympathy
and sorrow. The affecting pause was at length
broken by that prelate's inquiring in what manner
Sir Edward had been convinced of the prior
marriage ? When informed, again he paused :
Padre Anselmo, of Messina, was not unknown,
either as a lettered or a pious man, in Rome ;
and the cardinal was struck with chagrin to learn
that he had been the officiating priest at the fatal

ceremonial. Another long silence followed —
again broken by the cardinal, who, in a more
animated manner, inquired of Sir Edward if he
was sure that priest survived the earthquake? It
was a thought that had never occurred to the
exasperated father : yet, oh ! how comprehensive
was the possibility ! — the Marquis again lay
bleeding at his feet, — killed without reason,
perhaps; and his knees knocked together. The
cardinal, seeing in his agitation only anxiety, and
wholly unsuspicious of his self-accusation, assured
Sir Edward that there were records in the sacred
college of all the monks who had perished in the
convulsions of nature in Sicily; and he had a
wandering recollection of having seen Padre
Anselmo numbered among those swallowed up;
but he would be assured on this point ere they
met again. The discreet prelate took the farther
freedom of advising Sir Edward to be very wary
as to any step he might take respecting his
daughter's nuptials, and the consequent claims of
the Marquis's child by her; since it appeared to
him almost impossible for the base Miss Fitzallen
to authenticate her marriage; and nothing but her
doing that in the clearest and most unequivocal

manner could affect the rights of a lady of the same rank in life with the Marquis, regularly united to him, in the presence of her father, and with the full sanction of his own.

And now what became of Sir Edward, thus cruelly convinced, that, had he advised with one calm, rational, affectionate friend, he might perhaps have escaped whole years of anguish, and a life of conscious guilt? That he might henceforward be able to endure his own existence, he almost wished all inquiry on the painful subject stopt. It was some mitigation of misery and horror to believe the Marquis the greatest criminal. What would become of the wretched father, if he should be obliged to feel himself the only one?

The beneficent cardinal knew how to sympathise in sorrows which he had never personally felt; and saw, in the state of the unfortunate Marchioness of Lenox, a motive that quickened his diligence. The next day he hastened to confirm to Sir Edward the supposition he had formed. Padre Anselmo, with most of the fraternity, *had* been swallowed up with the great church, or buried in its ruins : and, to all human probability,

even if the rite of marriage had been regularly
performed between the Marquis and Miss Fitzallen, it was now become impossible for her to
establish any claim to his name or fortune; nor
would the church of Rome recognise or support
the assumptions of a worthless woman, only because she called herself a member of it, when
honour, justice, and the rights of an infant, born,
as it was obvious, either to ignominy, or to all that
gives distinction in society, even so outraged.

The wildest frenzy of soul preyed in silence,
as his friend spoke, upon Sir Edward Arden: he
—he himself then had eventually, as it appeared,
become but the most decisive implement of Emily
Fitzallen's vengeance; he, he, in the frenzy of the
hour had killed his nephew, and defamed his only
child, merely to accomplish those views which the
infamous woman, without the aid of his blind
passions, never could have accomplished.

From this horrible contemplation on the ruin
with which he had surrounded himself, Sir Edward
was roused by the cardinal's proposing to visit
Frescati, and comfort the youthful mourner with
the information that neither she, nor her daughter,
need shrink from that world in which their rights

were yet unquestionable. But here, again, by an error of judgment, Sir Edward interfered. He represented Emily, as she really was, in a very weak state, yet reconciled to her fate and the will of God, in its present form : but, as the discovery now made carried not conviction till confirmed by cautious inquiry, to awaken a hope, or quicken a pang in her bosom, might, as he feared, only tend to shorten the days which his benevolent friend wished to make long and peaceful. On the contrary, he thought it highly advisable, that they should both remain profoundly silent on the painful but important subject, for the present : while he, who had no use for life but to serve or save his daughter, would immediately embark for Messina ; where, by every inquiry which ingenuity could devise, both among the monks and the domestics of Count Montalvo, he would inform himself of such particulars as should ascertain the future rights of Emily and her infant, and prepare him to cope with the vindictive fiend whom he daily expected again to encounter.

The cardinal assured him that Rome was not the place Miss Fitzallen would be likely to choose for the scene of another exploit ; since the estimation

in which Sir Edward was held among the first
circle of learned men there, together with the rank
and merit of his unfortunate daughter, would
make it more probable that she should be shut up
in a dungeon as a licentious woman, than sanctioned in bringing forward any claim to the name or
fortune of the Marquis, were she daring enough
to announce that intention. The voyage of Sir
Edward his venerable friend, however, approved;
as well as the reasons he assigned for not com-
municating to the Marchioness the apparent prospect of her re-assuming rights so dear to herself,
so important to her child. — Alas! this was the
reasoning of man, and man only would so have
reasoned! The tender heart of woman would have
told her that the bleeding one of a lover might
break, while cool calculations of the future were
thus making.

Sir Edward, on returning to Frescati, found the
fair mourner still invisible from debility — an alien
still to comfort. Dr. Dalton, however, assured
him, that the symptoms of present danger had
disappeared, and it was possible she might recover.
This information enabled the anxious father
to prepare for his voyage with less reluctance.

In the projected inquiry was comprehended a hope soothing to his pride on Emily's account, though killing to his peace on his own. Yet, at whatever cost to himself, he felt it to be his duty to invest her again, if he had a conviction of no prior claim that could be established, with the title of which he had so madly robbed her. That once done, he intended immediately to set out with his whole family for England; where, placing Emily under the Duke of Aberdeen's protection, as the Marquis's widow, and having seen her child acknowledged as the heiress of both, he fully purposed to leave them; and, returning to Naples, expiate his sin, by mourning eternally on the grave of the Marquis; it seemed as if with that darling nephew he had lost his only tie to life, and its duties: nor could he hope ever more to associate with his daughter, since there sorrows, though equally powerful, were wholly distinct.

The bark that had conveyed the Marchioness to Cività Vechia was still lying there, and soon made ready to sail with Sir Edward Arden to Messina. Could he have known how ineffectual the anxious inquiries made by his unfortunate nephew on the same occasion had proved, never would he have visited the scene where all his miseries originated.

In sailing near the beautiful shore of Naples, the self-reproaching Sir Edward was strongly tempted to land; and on the spot where he had left the victim of his wrath, the beloved son of his beloved sister, weltering in his blood, to pour forth vain lamentations — eternal compunction : — but he conquered the impulse, resolving first to fulfil every duty to the living; when his embittered soul told him that he should consecrate all his future existence to bewailing the dead.

It seemed as if the air which Sir Edward had breathed had conveyed poison and death to the bosom of his miserable daughter; for, from the day he quitted Frescati, her fever decreased. Emaciated and dejected, she long continued; but her complaints no longer threatened to undermine her existence. With the dear increasing fondness of a mother, she watched over the last memorial of a husband whom she still adored; and the cares necessary for her own preservation she could only be prevailed upon to take by its being urged to her, that they were essential to the welfare of her daughter.

The villa inhabited by Emily was not large, but the grounds and gardens belonging to it inclosed variety of natural beauty, together with marble fragments of some vanished but memorable building, once seated on nearly the same spot. These gardens, though in a neglected disordered state, abounded with the rich and beautiful plants natural to the soil, and cherished by the softness of the climate. In this solitary domain Emily suddenly found herself sole sovereign, and explored its limits with a melancholy pleasure, which the grand contention of glowing nature with majestic, yet mouldering art, never fails to produce in a reflecting mind. The myrtles, vigorously emerging between narrow lines of fallen columns, and shedding their uncherished blossoms over the perishing works of man, brought home a thousand sad monumental ideas to the sick heart of Emily, and made it sometimes pause upon its sorrows. Amid this splendid wilderness, those sorrows acquired an influence doubly dangerous, as they now kindled into romance.

In the deepest shades, and by the cooling fountains with which the gardens abounded, antique statues, saved from the ruins still scattered around,

were fancifully disposed; some of these, though
injured, had originally been invaluable for the
design, no less than the execution. There is something in sculpture inconceivably touching to the
mind of sensibility, when deeply sunk in sorrow.
The almost breathing statue, while it unites the
chilling effect of death, with all the energetic graces
of life, diffuses a fearful holy kind of delight, that,
by a charm incomprehensible to ourselves, blends
the distinct impressions peculiar to each state ;
dilates our nature, and lifts the admiring soul
beyond the narrow bound of mortal breath and
mere existence.

These saddening contemplations aided the tender emotions of Emily's heart, where still the
Marquis reigned, though he lived no longer.
Fancy, at intervals, almost gave existence to ideal
objects. It is only those who have loved, and
loved even unto death, who find a freezing pleasure
in calling for ever the mouldering tenant of the
tomb before them ; and when the painfully-rational
consciousness will obtrude that he can no more
revisit earth, it is such only who " turn their
eyes inward, and behold him there."— No fear
enters the heart where perfect love has been ; and,

once more to behold her Edward, was, in the
depth of midnight, no less than the blaze of noon,
at every hour, and in every place, the wish, the
prayer, the sole desire of Emily.

From loathing Italy, and, above all, Frescati,
the melancholy that had now seized on Emily
made her partial to both. " Let my father return
to England by himself," cried she often to her
own heart, while she wandered. " The world
has still something for his proud mind; for me it
has nothing but the child of my Lenox, and his
ashes."

Emily, with her lovely infant, now almost lived
in the romantic and shady solitudes of Frescati;
where, as her lonely reveries at times broke into
invocation, her domestics began to apprehend,
that her mind, too highly wrought, was preying
upon itself, and melancholy might be taking the
distorted form of madness. Her musical instruments were laid in her way; but that once favourite science she now, with a kind of horror, rejected. Melody was become to her but the echo
of vanished pleasure; creative fancy had, however, supplied her a resource not less soothing, in
poetry; and to that internal music Emily began

insensibly to adapt the tender effusions of an overcharged heart.

The servants, thus gloomily occupied in watching over and commenting upon their lonely lady, found a contagious kind of horror insensibly creep over themselves. It was not long before it settled into a fear, which Emily could not but perceive : they dared not, after evening closed, venture over the threshold ; and, even in traversing the villa, usually moved in a body. The neighbourhood of Rome is not sufficiently secure for a lady to wander alone, after night falls, in solitary gardens ; and as Emily now found the aversion of her domestics to guarding her nocturnal rambles, became avowed, universal, and unconquerable, she was obliged to retire, when the day closed, to her own apartments ; and listening to the wind as it agitated the surrounding foliage, catch, through the breaks, imperfect glances at the ever-varying moon, and address to that the impassioned elegies which she past whole nights in composing.

It was soon whispered through the busy train of domestics, and fully credited, that their lady had at midnight a constant visitation from the spirit of the Marquis : nay, some were so daring as to affirm that they had heard his voice. Credulity is no less the characteristic of the vulgar Italians than Irish, and of these two nations was the household composed. It is true the former added superstition to credulity, and the latter soon resorted to it. Beads and relics became the reliance of all the servants in their hours of retirement; and liberal potations enabled them to hold out while in society with each other. As they all knew that their lady never took either of these modes of keeping up her spirits, they agreed one evening, that, unless they ingeniously devised some way of diverting her thoughts from the moon and the dead, she would soon be lost to all the purposes of existence. They recollected how fond she had formerly been of music; and as she always sat now with her windows open, they resolved magnanimously to venture in a body into the colonnade her apartment was over, to inspirit her with a lively strain. Some of the men were tolerable proficients; but the terror they were under, and the ignorance of the rest, made their nocturnal concert a most hideous performance. Yet their gentle mistress saw so much kindness in an effort, which she knew made the whole train of musicians tremble, that she had not the heart to show her sense of displeasure in any other way than by shutting her windows softly, whenever the miserable dissonance began. An intimation so delicate would not, however, have induced the servants to discontinue a practice that gave them importance with themselves, if not with their lady, when a hint of another kind not only silenced them for ever, but drove them into the house, over each other's backs, to apply to their beads, relics, and Pater-nosters. A low and heavenly melody one night suddenly issued from a lone hollow in the garden, not very remote, and entranced the listening Emily. Wild as the winds was the strain, yet harmonious as the spheres; eccentric, awful: the spot from whence too it appeared to come was romantic and singular: the ground in that part of the shrubbery sunk, with sudden, yet beautiful inequalities, into a deep dell, rich with bold rocks, and shadowed with lofty trees. In its hollow a translucent fountain sprang playfully up, and fell as playfully again; upon the farther side, on the rise of the velvet margin, was happily placed an antique statue of a Faun, who seemed surveying himself in the water as he

played on a pipe. The workmanship was so exquisite, that the charmed eye could almost believe
the graceful figure moved its arms, and gave
breath to the pipe on which its light fingers
rested.

Eagerly did Emily wait for the morning; when
she impatiently issued out to trace, if possible,
the nocturnal musician. From a Grecian temple
on the boldest of the brows overhanging the dell,
where Emily often passed whole days, she could
with ease survey the whole lovely scene. Her
eye, however, found in that no change. The
beautiful Faun touched his marble pipe with his
usual grace; but from it no sound issued. The
fountain still dimpled, with a pleasing murmur, the
pool which it formed; but no human foot was
imprinted on its margin. All that day, and many
a following one, did Emily pass in this favourite
temple, without seeing or hearing a living creature;
save the servants, who, with fear and trembling,
brought her at noon a light repast. As evening
came on, she would lift her beloved infant from
its downy bed, and return to her own apartment,
there to wait, with reverential awe, for the nocturnal visitation. Nor did it ever fail. Night after

night, irregular, but entrancing melody, soothed her sense, and sunk into her soul. The grand enthusiasm of her nature blending the hallowed charm of another world with those wild visions of this, which the nursery leaves on every mind, at times almost inclined her to believe her prayers were heard, and that Heaven had granted to her sorrowful soul a visionary intercourse with him whom it no longer permitted her to behold. Yet much she languished to know if mortal sense might not be allowed to discern the aërial harmonist, thus veiled in night. — To venture through the shades alone was, however, more than she dared do; not that fear withheld her: it was a solemn awe, which she thought it impiety to overrule. Bending from the window, she often fondly exclaimed, as to the spirit of her husband:

" Oh! vanished only from my sight,
While fancy hovers near thy urn,
And midnight stillness reigns, return ;
But no ethereal presence wear :
In the same form, so long belov'd, appear ;
Each woe-mark'd scene let me retrace,
And fondly linger o'er each mortal grace : —
Oh! strike the harp of heav'n, and charm my ear
With songs, that, worthy angels, angels only hear !"

Yet even thus invoked, no vision floated before that sense which strained to penetrate the thicket leading to the dell. The servants, forming as usual their own premises, and drawing their own conclusions, had, in full assembly, agreed, that this unaccountable music proceeded from the pipe of the Faun; and, for a very convincing reason, — that there certainly was nothing alive in the garden, and the Faun was the only musical performer, even in marble. That he was formed of no better materials they did not attempt to deny, whenever their gentle lady urged that conviction; but accounted for their own opinion, by in turn asserting, that the devil reigned, ever since the creation, from midnight to the break of day; and, during that interval, it was plain, animated the marble Faun, notwithstanding all the Aves and Pater-nosters they were constantly repeating: though, to their own pious diligence in that respect, they imputed his remaining still stationary. That they, however, might for ever continue in the same state of ignorance, as to whether the midnight musician was, or was not, the marble god, at the very first harmonious sound they heard in the dell, as at the stroke of a house-clock announcing the hour of rest, they all, with one consent, hastened to their beds; and tucking their heads under the clothes, past there the whole time of the solemn serenade : had the Faun therefore walked into the house, he might have walked over and out of it, without being seen by a single creature, save Emily; who, remaining ever at her window, listening, wondering, and weeping, pondered frequently on exploring this interesting solitude by herself. But, alas ! though she knew not how to fear any inhabitant of a better world, this yet contained one whom she was born to dread; — and Miss Fitzallen, too, excelled on the flute. If, by indiscreet curiosity, she should put herself into the power of that eternal foe of her peace, and rob her Edward's child of a last parent (for that was often the only, and ever the predominant consideration with Emily), how, how, should she be acquitted to God and the precious infant?

Yet the servants appeared to their lady to be correct in asserting the music not only came from the dell, but from the precise spot where the statue stood. There were moments, however, when she fancied it approached her; and others,

when, with sweet languishment, it sunk, as if retiring, into silence.

So deep a hold had this melancholy, visionary
delight, taken on Emily, that the days hung
heavily with her; and a restless impatience for
night became the habit of her mind : which, then,
no less eagerly awaited the mysterious indulgence.
Its period was as regularly announced by the wan
faces, and trembling steps of her domestics, as by
her own high-raised fancy and beating heart.   One
night of peculiar beauty, when the moon, with a
more pure and radiant lustre than usual, sailed
through the deep blue of a clear Italian sky,

> " When not a zephyr rustled through the grove,
>   And ev'ry care was charmed but guilt and love,"

Emily, as had long been her custom, stood at her
window, in fond expectation of the aërial music,—
it broke at once upon her ear as very, very near
her.   She started, turned round, as thinking it in
the chamber ; it was not behind her; she leaned
over, to seek it in the colonnade ; it was not
below. — From those vague, grand, and uncertain

strains, which she had been used to hear, the nocturnal musician wandered into one, dear to her heart, familiar to its beatings. She sprang up, and leaned from the window, with wild and increasing energy, — wrung her white hands, and called upon the invisible power of harmony to stand revealed before her; for this, she cried,

> " This is no mortal visitation, nor no sound
> That the earth owes."

Irresistibly impelled to trace the visionary charmer, she snatched the taper, and descending to the saloon, threw open the door, and found herself alone in the colonnade. Glancing her quick eyes in every direction, she saw only the long range of white marble pillars, half shadowed, and half shown by the trees and the moon. The music became more remote, low, faint, and, to her idea, ethereal; it seemed to retire towards the dell, and woo her thither. " It is, it can only be the shade of my Edward !" sighed Emily, resting her forehead on her arm, and that against a pillar, to save her from falling. " How often have I called thee from the grave, my love !" cried she: " and shall

I fear to follow thee even thither ?"——She tottered, her heart beating high, towards the winding path, which breaking the descent, led safely to the hollow glen.   Bright as the moon shone, it had hardly power to penetrate the thick foliage of the lofty trees, beneath which the trembling Emily lingered. No step, however, could she hear; no form could even her fluttered imagination fashion; yet still the music, with more melting sweetness, invited, and fearfully she followed.   On a point near the depth of the dell, the shade suddenly broke away, and disclosed the fountain, quivering to the moon which it reflected.   Though she knew not why she feared, Emily turned her eyes timidly towards the statue of the Faun.   What were her sensations, when she fancied she saw two resembling figures, one half shading the other !   A quickened second glance convinced her that this was no error of her sense ; overcome by surprise and terror she tried to save herself from falling, by grasping a tree, but sunk at its root.

From this temporary suspension of her faculties, Emily recovered, at the soft sound of a voice, that, to her impassioned sense, " might create a soul under the ribs of death."   The murmuring whis-

per of known endearment seemed to her the sweet
tone of the Marquis. The arms that, with fond
familiar pressure, supported her from resting on
the damp earth could, to her apprehension, be
only those by which alone she had ever wished
herself encircled. She fondly listened without
daring to unseal her eye-lids, lest the dear, the
cherished delusion, should vanish, and some hideous form, either living or dead, again harrow up
her nature. Still fondly urged to look up, by
many a whispered prayer and soft entreaty, she
at length timidly lifted her eyes to — Gracious
Heaven! could it be? — her husband? — the
Marquis himself! to her the single being in creation! Invigorated in a moment, she sprang up
with ethereal lightness, and the enraptured embrace, mutually given and received, repaid these
unfortunate lovers for all the miseries that had
marked their union. Too mighty was the ecstasy
to waste itself in words : again they gazed, again
embraced; they could only gaze, sigh, weep, and
murmur.

"Lives then my love?" cried Emily, at length :
"and has my cruel father, in wanton power, told
me otherwise only to torture me even to the

extremity?" — "That I live, soul of my soul," replied the Marquis, "your father neither knows, nor perhaps ever must know. Oh! Emily, *to* you, *for* you alone I live; be gracious then and hear me: allow me at last to pour forth all the secrets of my heart; to you, as to God, will I be sincere, and then shall my beloved decide my fate and her own. But this is a dangerous place for long discourse; the dews of night might prove fatal to so delicate a frame: — alas! my Emily is much changed, since we parted, by sickness and by sorrow." — "And you too, Edward," — Emily could not utter — "are not less changed." A gush of tears explained her meaning, and she hid the wan face her nature melted over in her bosom. Recovering herself, she took his hand: — "Come to my apartment, my love, nor fear any eyes, save mine, will observe you; terror, at this hour, closes all others in my house." — "Nor would seeing induce any of your domestics to follow me," replied her husband; "since, to win you to seek, and oblige them to shun me, was alike my object, in assuming a disguise that might yet, perhaps, startle my Emily, unless she coolly and collectedly surveys it." Emily cast her eyes in fond certainty

over his figure, as though in no disguise could it
ever shock or startle her; yet owned his tender
precaution was not unnecessary.   He was clothed
in a white vest, fitted close to his graceful form,
and exactly resembling the Faun; the mask, which
covered his whole head, with his flute, painted
alike white, he held in his hand.   When, at her
desire, he put the artificial head-piece on, it was
sufficiently clear that he might encounter her
whole family, and not be known to any one of
them for a being of this world.

Conducted by his wife through the saloon to
her apartment, the Marquis once more removed
the mask; and Emily, still unsatisfied with gazing,
fixed on him again her fond eyes with deep in-
tentness, as even then doubting whether the bless-
edness of the moment were not a vision, or the
dear hand she clasped might not, while yet she
held it, become marble.

During this affecting silence, each lover too
visibly perceived what it was to have lost the
other.   The Marquis, still pale, even to lividness,
from the effusion of blood in his duel, was greatly
debilitated by the half-healed wound, which obliged
him to lean to the right side.   Emily soon dis-

covered this new claim to her tenderness; and abhorring the necessary disguise, felt it as a great relief, that she had hoarded, among the treasures sacred to his memory, a part of his wardrobe, often kissed and sprinkled with her tears. She refused to hear a word till she had seen him comfortably arrayed, and resting his aching side on a sofa; then taking the posture in which he had implored her to allow him to pour forth his soul, the tender Emily threw herself on her knees by the couch, and filled up the pauses pain and fatigue occasioned in his narration, by prayers and devout ejaculations to the God who had graciously preserved, and thus miraculously restored him to her.

The Marquis now required not a moment to methodise his recital; he had no past thought to conceal, no wish to leave untold. He began the detail, that sunk into Emily's soul, at the period when the persecuting fiend first gained his pity and protection at Paris. His wife heard the name of Hypolito with comparatively little emotion; for she was fully assured of her own boundless empire over a heart which she ever, till this moment, believed she had divided with that youth and Miss

Fitzallen; for only now did she understand that
they were one and the same person. He described the talents and tastes of the impostor, so
naturally consonant and studiously adapted to his
own, and the influence gained by the feigned
youth in his affections. The ingenuous nature of
Emily made her instantly allow that it must be
almost an impossibility for any man to escape so
secret and near an attack from a lovely woman,
unrestrained in the pursuit of her object by either
virtue or feeling. He, in the most natural manner, painted the discovery made of her disguise
at Messina; and bewailed the wandering, both of
his senses and his reason, by the fever of wine
and of passion. But, oh ! how the gentle Emily
started and wept, lamenting, too late, her own
innocent romance as the daughter of Dennis;
when she learnt that, and that only, could have
enabled her ingenious and base enemy to add, to
her own dangerous allurements, the assumption
of her name, character, and rights in life. How
strange appeared it to the tender wife to find that
the Marquis had married, or meant to marry, her
in the person of another. She was lost in horror
at the awful catastrophe of the earthquake; though

her heart was more lightened than she chose to own, at finding that it had prevented the Marquis from consummating his mistaken and miserable marriage. The agony he felt at the deplorable fate of the fair impostor; his subsequent and sorrowful researches for the dear supposed daughter of Sir Edward Arden:—all, all appeared natural, touching, and hardly questionable, to the generous spirit to which he was now appealing.—Emily's own heart now took up the tale. The moment of their meeting in Switzerland, the gay discovery of herself, she then meditated; and the shock it appeared to give him, to be told that she was the daughter of Sir Edward Arden, Emily well remembered. The hours of unalloyed pleasure that followed, till the hapless one arrived that united their hands, she never could forget. The frenzy that then seized the hapless Lenox he fully accounted for, in representing to her the impressive spectre that extended to him the ring, on the steps of the portico, and annihilated, at once, their bridal happiness. The scene lived with equal force before Emily's eyes, as she read, in the wild glances of his, the eternal impression made on his mind by that horrible moment. Oh !

how generous, how noble, how pure, appeared, to her informed judgment, that mysterious coldness and constraint, which, at the time, had so shocked, — perhaps secretly offended her. She now, however, would again interrupt him; nor would longer allow him to be his own historian : her delicate nature made her anxious to spare him all further mention of Miss Fitzallen; who, hard and self-loving, had, it was obvious, wrung from him, through the medium of his fears, those rich baubles which she in the exultation of malice every where displayed — nor doubted the generous Emily, but that her little favourite carriage had been obtained by the same insolent exaction.

But much, much yet remained for Emily to learn and to feel, when the Marquis, straining to his heart the generous creature who would not allow him to accuse himself, and melting under the sad blessing of her tearful forgiveness, faintly uttered — " Oh ! Emily, adored of my soul ! had your harsh father thus treated me — I should perhaps in bitterness of spirit have shed at his feet my own blood, and spared him the horror of having poorly satisfied his vengeance with stretching me there." — This was a thought with which the tender wife had not ventured to trust her own soul : — the idea spread at first through the family, that, in a fit of phrensy, the Marquis had rashly ended his sufferings, had by means of her woman immediately reached Emily; and, horrible as such a fate must be, it was less dreadful than the faintest apprehension that her father had shortened the days of his nephew, and that she should be for life compelled to implore a blessing from the hand yet crimson with her husband's blood, or claim protection from the heart, hard enough to render her a widow, and her unborn babe fatherless. — The intelligence from Naples, afterwards sent by Cardinal Albertini, the valet of Sir Edward, had officiously circulated in the family; and Emily dared not trust herself to make any minute inquiry upon the agonizing subject, nor needed an exact account, to figure to herself all the horrors of his fate.

She in turn described to the Marquis the sudden manner, and the means, by which she had been decoyed, as it were, from Naples — and her memorable meeting with her father at Frescati; when, in the ungoverned state of his feelings, he was incapable of reflection, and in-

sensible to pity. — She repeated, in all the force
in which the words dwelt on her mind — " *You
have no husband — you never had one !*" and her
impulsive shudder proved too plainly that Sir
Edward for ever lost at that moment the affection
of his daughter. — The haughtiness with which
he had ordered, without her consent, that she
should be deprived of the title of the Marquis,
lived no less in her memory; and finally the
severe justice by which he had outraged every
feeling, in obliging her to provide for her innocent babe in case of her own death, by a will
which stigmatized the infant's birth, was too
wounding to be unmentioned. — That nice sense
of female delicacy, which speaks even in silence,
made Emily by intuition convey to her husband's
heart a deep resentment at these repeated indignities, while both overlooked the mortifying exi-
gencies by which they were caused, nor could
allow the father to be an equal, perhaps, as the
proudest of the three, the greatest sufferer. —
This union of grievances strengthened every other,
and the hearts of the only two beings on earth
whom Sir Edward Arden really loved, agreed,
while they renewed to each other the sacred vow

of eternal tenderness and faith, in shutting him entirely out, and utterly rejecting him.

After an interval, the Marquis resumed his narration — " Left in the garden of the convent, drowned in my own blood, and to all human appearance dead, — or even your incensed father would not so have left me, — many hours must have elapsed before any of the brotherhood wandered that way. I faintly recollect, that it was torch-light when the pain I felt in their lifting me on a mattress, to convey me to the convent, caused me for a moment to open my eyes — Delirium and impending death were long, long, my portion, in the lonely cell where the benevolent monks attended me with unremitting care ; one of them, who had been an eminent surgeon, dressed my wound with tender skill : — nor, in the intervals of my raving, when the agony of my mind made that of my body forgotten, did the pious fathers omit all those holy attentions, so comforting to the wretch in this world, so necessary to prepare him for a better. — I easily understood by the tenor of their consolations, that they regarded me as a frantic creature, who with rash hand had sought to end my own calamities. — I found a sad

R 3

consolation in saving my inhuman uncle from censure, and never gave any other answer to the inquiries which the superior ventured, as soon as he saw me likely to recover, than that the fatal catastrophe had been caused by my own despair : and that, unless they meant to drive me to the same extremity a second time, they would conceal from every human being, even my nearest relations, or tenderest friends, my continued existence. Upon this condition, and this condition only, would I promise to endure my fate.

" In the miserable state of my health, and the frantic irritation of my mind, the benignant brotherhood held it wise to yield to every request that might conciliate my feelings, or mitigate those complicated sufferings which were perhaps an ample punishment for my sin, great as I own it — and by this indulgence was I won still to suffer.

" I soon learned that Sir Edward had quitted Naples with you; nor doubted, as the monks affirmed no inquiries had been made for me, that you, even you, my Emily, were wholly governed by his impression of my conduct, and turned from my very grave with abhorrence. Oh! misery,

never to be understood but by the wretch who has,
like me, felt it; to find all the sacred ties which
reason, fancy, feeling, can form, and choice sanc-
tify, burst with a force that throws you a solitary
sufferer to the utmost limits of creation! When
I remembered Emily was mine no more — no
more wished to be mine — it would have been
happiness indeed to die. My infant too — my
dear unborn — the cruel Sir Edward could not
teach *that* to shrink from my embrace — to close
its little ears to my lamentations. But the child
of my Emily was like herself to be torn from me;
and I stood alone in the universe.

"My imbittered spirit for a time soured me to
all soft impressions; and the deep gloom of my
abode co-operated to lead my thoughts only to
monastic seclusion. By annihilating myself in a
manner, and yet enduring the sufferings I had
brought upon my own head, I thought I might in
a degree expiate my sin against Emily and her
father, and perhaps obtain the pardon of Heaven.
But, with the least improvement of my health,
silence, solitude, La Trappe, disappeared from
my eyes — love and Emily still throbbed at my
heart, and incurable tenderness was blended there

with a grief no less incurable. — Alas! had I not
cause to dread a resentment on her part at least
equal to that of her inexorable father, though she
would not show it in the same bloody manner? I
often felt myself sinking into the grave, under the
curses of both. Yet were there moments when
her angel-form appeared before me with all that
softness which renders her sway so absolute. — I
sometimes seemed to see her mourning for the
very wretch who had marked her days with ignominy and affliction, and clasping to her snowy
bosom with increased fondness, because springing
from me, the infant-inheritor of both. Returning strength (though I was still very weak) impressed with more force this cherished idea. I
resolved, the moment I was able, to venture into
the country where my adored Emily had fixed her
abode, and there meditate on the mode by which
I might acknowledge, even to the extent, my of-
fences against her, and make her judge, sole judge,
in her own cause.

" I had not patience to wait till my wound was
healed; crawling only half alive, as yet, on the
face of the earth, I assumed the habit of a common labourer, and found a neighbouring peasant

with whom I could abide. I told him my employment was that of a mason, and the hurt in my
side was occasioned by the sudden fall of a frag-
ment, as I was hewing marble : that the weakness
which the accident brought on had long threatened
a consumption ; and, now I was able to get abroad,
I had been advised to try whether the pure air of
Frescati would not remove the alarming symptoms.
I might have added, that if not, in his poor cottage should I end my days. I had reason to think
their termination at hand, when I there had the
misery to be told that my wife had again taken the
name of Miss Arden ; and the infant she cherished
in her arms was not allowed to bear that of its
father. Yet, I learned the precious infant lived !
it was mine, my Emily, no less than yours ; how
did I languish to behold you both ; and to claim
my fond, fond right, in our mutual treasure.
Night after night did I pass in wandering round
the consecrated abode of my Emily, and ponder-
ing upon the possibility of conveying a letter to
her. Yet a single indiscretion might be ruin,
even if I moved her compassion. Sir Edward
would not, it was true, again strike at my existence in my own person ; but, alas ! he had it in

his power even more effectually to do it in the person of his daughter. The cruel predicament I stood in took from me the right of a father : —— that of a husband I dared not claim. It was only the gentle heart of Emily would grant me either, and to that heart I felt I must appeal or die.

" In exploring the limits of the wilderness, I one day found a little aperture; through which, the following night, I made my way, and boldly passed into the garden. My sick soul seemed to revive, when I breathed the same air with my Emily; and these nocturnal rambles became an exquisite indulgence. One night I could not resist approaching so near the house, as to see my uncle walking about in his chamber, and sometimes standing at the window : the lights were behind him, and I plainly discerned his figure —— never, never can the strange, the complicated feeling escape my memory — that form, always so natural to my eyes — once so dear, so very dear to my heart ! — A frantic kind of emotion came over me; I felt ready to cry out — to demand — to extort his pity — perhaps to undo myself — and not only lose for ever my Emily, but rob her of the little tranquillity which my fatal love had left her. — That I might no more risk so exquisite a temptation, I withdrew to Rome in the hope Sir Edward would soon depart.

" In wandering, as I often did, whole days there among the colossal fragments of ancient magnificence, a fallen and mutilated statue of a Faun caught my eye, and recalled to my mind the one I had seen by the fountain. The strange project of procuring, under the idea of wearing it at a masquerade, a habit exactly resembling the statue, then occurred to me. I had often apprehended meeting some of your domestics, whom curiosity or love might lead to wander at the same hour in the garden; but, thus hid, I was sure of having it all to myself. This disguise being prepared, I again housed with my peasants; and, such is the energy of even a remote hope, was flattered by them on my improved looks. — Sir Edward Arden was at last gone; and his lovely daughter, whom they touchingly termed the melancholy lady, left alone. Now then, or never, I must obtain the sight of my Emily; and, a month ago, when the moon shone with the same brightness it does at this moment, assuming my disguise, I hid my own clothes in the grotto in the wilderness; then, without fear, sought the deep dell, to survey my fellow sylvan. How exquisitely beautiful appeared the silent scene! The temple, hanging on the rude brow above, had now the windows thrown open. I made no doubt but that my beloved had been sitting there. I stole through the shady path, and, after listening intently, finding all was solitude, ventured an intrusion. Think of the melting softness that seized my heart, on beholding the sofa my love had so lately quitted; and on which a basket of her work yet remained! I knelt and worshipped, as if the fair form I adored was still reposing there. On the ground were scattered flowers, which, as perishing, she had cast from her bosom. I gathered them up, as devout pilgrims do holy relics, and thrusting them into mine, bade them thus return to Emily!

"An emotion, new — sacred — eternal, yet remained for me to experience, when I cast my eyes on a large wicker basket quilted with down, and covered with a mantle. Softly I raised that covering, as though the jewel were yet enshrined within it. The cradle was empty; yet on the pillow still remained the dear, the soft impression of my infant's tender cheek. That inanimate pillow was wet with the first tears of a father — greeted with his kisses — consecrated by his blessings. I remained riveted to a spot enriched with such interesting local remembrances. I could not resolve to quit it ; and, in that sanctuary of innocence, the cradle, had half resolved to hide, for my Emily's observance, some known memorial of our plighted love ; when a sound that suddenly reached me, of " riot and rude merriment," suggested a better mode of attracting her. I guessed this rustic serenade to be some mode of amusement, which your servants had found for themselves ; and they had repeated the discordant strains several evenings before I discovered that it was meant to entertain you. I then coloured my flute to correspond with my dress ; and in the depth of night, silenced the savages with my lonely pipe. At intervals I paused, to listen whether curiosity had brought too near my retreat any of my auditory. Not a step could I ever hear : not a whisper reached me.

" Night after night I pursued my wild symphonies, always apprehending that some one of the domestics, bolder than the rest, would pierce the thicket, to descry my haunt : but convinced no second person would venture near it. Your people were all, however, equally timorous ; and this beautiful solitude I now feared would ever belong at night only to my brother sylvan and myself. Assured that I had cleared it of all my vulgar hearers, I soon became bolder, and ventured from behind the marble Faun. Sometimes I could see your shadow in your dressing-room — sometimes knew it could be only you at the window. Yet some person might be in the room, and one incautious word have betrayed me. I almost despaired of wooing you into the garden, when, this evening, I suddenly called to mind that little air which your tender heart so feelingly acknowledged. When I saw the effort successful — when the light disappeared from the room above, and faintly began to illumine the Colonnade — when I found that love, stronger than death, could win my Emily to follow even my supposed phantom, my heart no longer feared hers. — Alas ! I feared only the alarm, which it was impossible to spare her, ere she could be again encircled in those arms that never, never more will resign her, even to her father."

In discourse like this, whole ages might have elapsed, unheeded by the Marquis; but Emily, exquisitely alive to his danger, now saw with affright that day had, unobserved, stolen upon them, and it was impossible for him, disguised or otherwise, to return through the garden. The Marquis made light of his stay or departure; for, if she approved the former, who should object? but, on the soul of Emily, the fear of her father was now incurably impressed: and all their future views were too uncertain, and indistinct to both, for her husband to urge a rash discovery. He therefore permitted her to conduct him, through her own, to the vacant apartment of Sir Edward; where, having fastened the entrance at the extremity, she insisted on his endeavouring to recruit his emaciated frame by needful rest; and, locking the intermediate chamber, retired to repair her own strength and spirits with a balmy slumber. How different was this day from the last, when, waking, she felt happiness once more possible. The husband whom she adored, ever faithful, though apparently otherwise, was for life her own. With light elastic footstep, a hundred times in the course of the day did she visit the door that divided them. As often did she softly pace back again, and fearfully shrink from the indulgence of even looking upon her beloved. Once, and once only, did she unlock it, and impatiently wait to see him partake of the refreshments which she carried him.

The approaching evening, Emily purposed, should afford the Marquis the exquisite pleasure hardly more desired by him than herself — the sight of their infant. Affecting an alarm, she took it from the charge of the nurse, to place it for that night in her own bed. Let those who have borne a child to an absent husband tell the soft exultation which nature makes powerful enough to compensate the pang that renders them mothers, when they lift the sheltering mantle of the sleeping innocent, to show to the father those features in which each parent, by a magic of mind, discerns only the likeness of the other, combined with the charm peculiar to infancy ! — Sorrow — sickness — the past — the future — all was forgotten by the Marquis and Emily, when, with sweet contention, kneeling together, they blessed and kissed this dear third in their union.

Who can fail to lament, that a nature so generous and susceptible as Sir Edward Arden's should have lost, by one start of ill-judged passion, the dear delight of sharing a bliss which it had been the single object of his life to ensure to the two so exquisitely endeared to him ? — Occupied wholly by gloomy reflections, and a hopeless pursuit, Sir Edward was wandering, without one social bosom in in which to confide a thought, through the scenes in Sicily most afflicting to his remembrance : nor had he been able to gather any further information concerning the monks, who had been immediately parties in the ceremony of the Marquis's marriage, than that Padre Anselmo certainly perished ; but it was doubtful in what quarter of the world the survivors might now be seeking means to rebuild a part of their convent.

Hours, days, and months, fly swiftly to those who love, and love happily. In the nocturnal interviews which the Marquis and Emily still mysteriously carried on, they had ever so much to say of the past and present, that both, as by tacit agreement, threw as far off as possible the more important and immediate consideration of the future. The full confession and explanation of the Marquis had removed every fear of impropriety from the mind of Emily. It was to her sufficiently clear, that nothing but the pride and ungovernable fury of her father prevented the previous ceremony that had been read to the Marquis and Miss Fitzallen (since it was a mere ceremony), from being, when submitted to ecclesiastical discussion, declared, if not informal, certainly invalid ; while her own marriage, celebrated with the consent of the parents on both sides in the face of the world, and by every rite of her own church, had the full confirmation of her having borne a child whom it would be impossible to deprive of legitimacy, when its claims were duly made. It was no new vow, therefore, on the part of Emily, to follow her husband through the world; but she exacted, in consideration of this concession, that he should allow her to do it in her own way.

The Marquis, who had long found his love for his uncle on the wane, had likewise long felt all fear of him vanish. He was fully sensible that Sir Edward had no authority over his daughter's person, if once she could be influenced to assert a will of her own, and abide by her marriage. He sometimes almost wished accidental circumstances would, by betraying their secret correspondence, oblige her to a decision which even he found it a vain attempt to urge her to fix. Nothing, he was assured, was so likely to effect this, as the dread of their separation; and were his nocturnal visits once known, she would have no choice but to fly with him, and thus compel her father to second their views. Yet, delicately as Emily was situated — delicately as she ever felt — to *force* her to any thing would, he was very conscious, be so ungenerous a procedure, that the Marquis suffered the happy hours to steal on, without forming any fixed plan for the future.

That time, however, had a consequence so favourable to his views, so gratifying to his heart, that he rejoiced he had never, by word or thought, grieved his Emily. Terrified — pale — dying in a manner with fear — she threw herself one evening into his arms, and whispered, " that the child he then clasped to his bosom was not the only one it would be her misfortune to bring him." To all his soothing endearments, she only cried out in agony — " How, how should she ever face her father? He, who had already when she was in the same state, nearly killed her with his eye-beam, would now wound her with a sense of shame, (even while she was unconscious of of guilt,) too humiliating to be endured. Never, never, could she again encounter, thus circumstanced, the severity of her father. The Marquis, softened with the occasion of this anguish — shocked at seeing its excess — and ever yielding to her wishes — intreated, conjùred her to compose herself; solemnly vowing, that, whatever line of conduct would give most ease to her mind, should be that by which he would implicitly abide by, as the only atonement he could make for having a single moment exposed her, in the most interesting of all situations, to the indignity of her father's looks.

" Never, never, will I again encounter such a hateful feeling, my Edward," cried she with increasing affliction, " while there is either a spot to be discovered on the earth to hide this wretched head in, or a grave to be found beneath it. — I have sometimes thought — yet that would be very difficult — imposes upon you years — perhaps a life of seclusion — total annihilation of our rights, — shall I, poorly to save my own feelings, bury with me, while yet living, the heir of high rank and splendid fortunes ; with every charm and talent that shall make him a grace to his equals, a blessing to his dependants?"

"Emily," returned the Marquis, with a sweetly-sad solemnity, "I am yours — as we are circumstanced, yours only : no duty can come in competition with that which I owe to the angel whom my love has unhappily humbled, but never could elevate. Imagine my impatience, and tell me all those expressive eyes are full of."

"I have only a few valuables, and no money," continued Emily, as if thinking aloud, rather than speaking to any body. "Sold, as they must be, to a disadvantage, I could hardly hope they would produce more than three thousand pounds."

"Sell your ornaments, love?" returned the Marquis, in a tone of chagrin, as well as surprise : — "what for? — I have money to the amount you mention."

"Ah! Edward, we shall want that too," cried his wife, surveying him with a mournful steadiness, as doubting whether she had influence enough to bend the pride of his nature to the humble purpose of her heart.

"And what," cried the Marquis with some

quickness, " can my Emily want so large a sum for ? — To endow an hospital ?"

" No !" replied she, in a firm voice, and with a dignity of mien that gave her new charms in the eyes fondly fixed on her. "All we can both gather will be hardly enough, perhaps, to maintain us during the life of my father. You have bound yourself, my lord : — thus must it be, if I am again yours. Dare you, on these terms, confirm your vows ? Dare you take this hand, and swear on it, never, never to risk the little peace we now enjoy, by putting it in my father's power to tear us asunder ? Yet do not imagine that I am without pity, any more than you, for his future fate ; neither can I forget that in going I only take from him what he has shown me to be without value in his eyes — my wretched self."

" Oh ! Emily," returned her husband in tender agitation, " think well, think often, before you finally determine on a point so important. You will not, in this, accuse me of the indelicacy of considering myself. I am a man ever retired in my taste, nor expensive in my pleasures. I could easily reconcile myself to the inconveniences of humble life, did I not feel acutely for you ; but, born as you are to immense fortunes, bred on the bosom of luxury, yourself the most fragile and tender of nature's productions, can you endure to inhabit an humble home, and perhaps be hardly able, even by severe economy, to keep that ? How will you bear to see your little ones, who will be naturally entitled to every advantage, confined to a narrow spot and limited education."

" There was a time, my love," returned Emily, bitterly weeping, " when, vainly exulting in the advantages of nature and fortune, we both thought, that among the many modes of being happy, each of us might make a choice. Already that vision has vanished ; and all the option that now remains to either, is, what kind of suffering we can best bear. It is my fixed determination never more to endure that of meeting my unkind father : nor," sobbed she, throwing herself into his arms, " of parting with you."

The Marquis pressed her to his heart, but was not collected enough to reply. Emily continued :

" And why, Edward, should we think ourselves poor with the sums mentioned ? Fear not

but that I can descend to minute economy without murmuring; for I have feelingly learnt that
the splendour of an equipage relieves not the re-
pining heart — the gaudy drapery of a dress dries
not the tearful eye. In waving for a time our
claims in life, we neither renounce them for ourselves nor our children. The day will come when
the Duke of Aberdeen may recover his son: it is
Sir Edward Arden," faltered she, bursting anew
into a passion of tears, " who, by lifting his hand
against your life, and embittering mine — it is he
who has for ever lost his daughter."

The Marquis saw with tender distress the deep
impression which Emily's mind had taken; for to
oppose her in her present delicate state, it was
plain, would endanger, perhaps shorten, her life.
Yet, as a man, he calculated at a higher rate than
his retired, his gentle wife, the advantages which
they mutually inherited; and felt, that to partake
them was, from the hour of their birth, the right
of their children. One bold struggle with Sir
-Edward Arden would fix their fate. Could
Emily be won from a fear and delicacy so erroneous, the moment her father knew she had confirmed the rights of her husband, and meant to

pass her life with him, that very pride, which had disgracefully torn them asunder, would act for them, and urge him to assist every process which would establish their marriage. The Duke too, though not a tender parent, had never been an unkind or ungenerous one. To deprive him of natural ties, and the hope, always so dear to those declining in life, of seeing posterity around him, was very painful to the Marquis. Yet all these rational considerations faded from his mind, whenever he discussed this point with Emily; and the single one, that she might die, while her father and he were struggling how to reconcile their modes of making her great and happy, rendered him unable to oppose a project which he daily became more certain was not new to her thoughts, but the long cherished object of them.

Many concurring circumstances could alone enable Emily to execute the extraordinary project of vanishing for ever from her father's eyes; while a very simple event would render it totally abortive. Sir Edward's suddenly returning to Frescati; which appeared to both the lovers equally probable, and obliged the fearful Emily to resolve upon immediately sounding the two persons whom she had, in her mind, fixed on as confidants and auxiliaries. The first of these was her own woman. Mrs. Connor had waited on Lady Emily before she married Sir Edward Arden; had affectionately watched her in the sickness that laid her early in the grave; and remained in charge of the heiress of Bellarney till ripened youth allowed Emily to feel her power of acting for herself. From that moment the servitude of Connor was of her own choice. Not being, however, entitled to rank among Miss Arden's friends, and quite unable to live without some share of her society and regard, the worthy creature had preferred attending on her lady to the kind offer made by her of independence and her own way. These humble friends are among the peculiar blessings the Irish may boast; as if the high polish of cultivation gave hearts so very smooth a substance, that every object slid over them; while, in those more rough, there remained an adhesive power, which fixed whatever it once attracted. Natures of the latter cast have too often a generous defect in their coarse but strong perceptions of the injuries offered to those they

love, which to the sufferer magnifies the evils reflection would otherwise diminish.

Let no one say they are proof against this insensible operation of mind on mind. The wise
would be wise indeed, were they not liable to be
biassed by the weak; but it requires a great effort
to silence the voice of kindness, even if you think
the speaker not wholly competent to his subject.
Connor had all this secret and insensible influence
over her lady; and a horror of the lofty character
of Sir Edward Arden, which made her give the
most chilling interpretation to his words, the most
irritating one to his actions. She was among
those to whom he gave the " imperial" (as she
termed it) command, to call the wife of the Marquis of Lenox, Miss Arden. He had not thought
it proper, or necessary, to assign his reason for
this; and, had he commanded the good woman
to lay down her own existence, she could not
have been more determined never to comply; till
the gentle Emily, with tears, requested that her
father might be obeyed. From that moment,
Mrs. Connor persisted in it he would be the death
of that angel his daughter, hourly bewailing the
day he had ever set foot in Bellarney, and carried

away its young heiress to become a martyr to his whims, and know only sickness and sorrow. If any thing had been wanting to complete her detestation of Sir Edward, he would have supplied it, when he refused to see the " dear jewel," his grand-daughter, on the sad day of her birth. All the erroneous opinions of a woman, really worthy, were, however, from the succeeding danger of Emily, lost and swallowed up in her fears. No mother could be more watchfully tender; and, perhaps, but for even her unrefined attention, Sir Edward Arden's daughter had never survived her sickness at Frescati. As, however, her lady amended, by slow degrees Connor discharged her mind of its chagrins, which sunk into the already wounded soul of Emily, and produced the deepest horror of her father.

How dangerous is it for parents, in any station, to make over the care of their children, from an early age, to others! Of the tie so necessary to both, as they advance into life, nothing then remains, even in minds well turned, but a sense of mutual duty. The melting look that cherished an infant virtue, the tear that eradicated an infant fault, has never been riveted on the fond remembrance of the child. The sweet endearments, the soft concessions, which made every fault forgotten, the gay delights of unfolding nature, live not in the doating recollection of the parent. But when children inherit fortunes and rights in life, independent of their parents, it becomes peculiarly necessary for those parents to fix that influence, by early and unremitting kindness, which even the most insensible will lament the want of, whenever the younger party is entitled to judge and act.

Little did the Marquis suspect the great influence of Connor with Emily, or that she was meditating to commit to her sole charge the second dear treasure of her life. But the person she thought it most important to embark in her views, she knew, as yet, only from the friendly sensibility with which he soothed her sorrows; while, with exquisite professional skill he had perhaps saved her life.

Dr. Dalton had, to oblige Sir Edward, broken through the rule he laid down, when he took up his abode in Rome, never to practise, but for the benefit of those who were unable to reward him.

This gentleman was beyond the middle of life, easy in his own fortune, and married to a lady of a still ampler one. His taste for the fine arts had made him abandon his own country, to fix his residence in the centre of the ancient world; the venerable reliques of which formed his only pleasure. A man of this character could not but be courted by strangers; and Sir Edward Arden had made on him so favourable an impression, that he always took pleasure in being his *Cicerone*. Such a friend, with medical knowledge, became a treasure to the afflicted father, in the desperate contingence that followed Emily's arrival at Frescati. Her bitter grief, her exquisite loveliness, the disposition she showed to be grateful for his generous exertions to continue that existence which avowedly she valued not, had interested Dr. Dalton's feelings; and urged him to improve the predilection, by bringing his lady to wait on her. But in the melancholy and humbled situation of Emily, the deep dejection of her mind, and the weakness of her health, the good Doctor wondered not at her shrinking even from this mark of respect and kindness; when therefore he found his medical assistance un-necessary, he had no choice, but to retire from the

interesting young widow. Sir Edward had, however, obtained his promise, ere he left Rome, that,
if invited to Frescati, he would still attend on his
daughter.

The present interesting situation of Emily, inclined her from prudence to shun Dr. Dalton's
presence; and her loveliness was never more obvious. For herself, therefore, she could not sum-
mon the person whom she most desired to see.
The infant Emily was a cherub in beauty, and in
the full glow of health; and to trouble a man of
independence, with making a visit to two of her
servants who happened to be indisposed, seemed
too great a liberty: yet rendering their poverty an
excuse to his benevolent mind, she risked entreat-
ing her father's friend to visit Frescati.

Dr. Dalton obeyed the requisition, and con-
gratulated his fair patient on having recovered a
higher degree of health than he thought she ever
did or could possess. Her beautiful child delighted
him; and he assured her he could not any longer
contend with the impatience of his wife to see
both. Emily smiled, but no longer declined the
compliment. The Doctor returned, however, from
visiting her Irish domestics, with an air of gravity;

and not moving from a window remotely situated, inquired if she had ever had the small-pox. Emily replied, it was a disputed point between Connor and her grandmother; but the former could be called, and give him her reasons for thinking she had had it. "A simple proceeding will spare a long detail," said the kind physician. "Even if *you* have had this disorder, your little angel has not; and she must avoid the present imminent danger. Your two servants have taken the small-pox, and no human care can prevent its spreading among your Italian domestics. I shall, therefore, wave Mrs. Dalton's waiting on you, madam, and fulfil my promise to Sir Edward, by insisting on your company to Rome. My house is pleasantly situated, — the gardens are large, — your babe will there be safe, if she has not already received the infection, and anxiously attended if she has. This is a contingence when ceremony must be given up, and the old fashioned thing, called prudence, only govern us."

A thousand anxious thoughts fluttered at the heart of Emily, and varied her complexion every moment. Could she have guessed the present contingence, she might have previously apprised the Marquis; but to go without his knowledge was impossible; nevertheless, keeping her darling within the reach of infection, and the dread of death, she could not answer to herself. To the kind urgency of her medical friend, she with great hesitation replied, that some very particular concerns rendered it impracticable for her so suddenly to quit Frescati; but the babe, dearer to her than life, she would tear from her own arms, and commit immediately to his care, as a pledge that she would follow to-morrow. Dr. Dalton then ordered a horse to be made ready for himself; and Connor, with the infant Emily, and her nurse, drove at once off in his carriage.

For a time, the tender mother felt as if stunned. She ran from room to room seeking the babe whom she knew she could not find; and half fancying that she should never see it more. A new and pleasing idea then took full possession of her mind; and she past the interval, ere she could greet the Marquis, in collecting and packing all her valuables; appreciating each jewel, as she enfolded it, with a miser's eye. That done, she measured the room for hours, dreading lest some accident had happened to her dear nocturnal visitant; though her watch assured her it was yet too early for his appearance; — not but he might safely have ventured; for the nature of the malady which had seized the sick servants threw the deepest dismay over those yet in health, insomuch that each fancied himself walking about the house in a dying state; nor failed to conclude, that the memorable music of the marble Faun had been a solemn warning of the approaching mortality in the family.

When Emily apprized the Marquis of the imminent danger that had obliged her to part with her child, she soon saw his parental anxiety was not inferior to her own.   A moment, however, impressed him with a conviction, that this removal would involve them both in much inconvenience. Dr. Dalton, he perceived, was, by this hasty confidence, rendered of necessity a party in all their future prospects and fluctuating plans.   " What, my dearest," cried he, impatiently pacing the chamber, " could induce you so suddenly to impose such severe restraint on yourself and me? If you will not consent to my appearing, how can you reside at Dr. Dalton's house?   What will you do there?" — " Die, perhaps," returned

Emily; "I would not, my love, be understood
literally; yet to be thought dead is my only chance
for passing my life with you: and without the aid
of a character, as respectable in itself, and as
highly estimated by my father, as Dr. Dalton's,
vainly should I attempt an imposition of that
kind." — "How improbable then is it that you
should persuade such a man to sanction so strange
a fraud, and one which so many various occurrences in life may betray!" — "I know not any,
save choice, that can betray us, my lord," sighed
Emily; "and I will rather die in reality than
ever again endure the severe controul of my
father. I have well digested my plan, in which
I do not ask your aid; grant only your concurrence; and this, if I am indeed dear to you,
I may claim. The circumstances in which I find
myself are interesting and peculiar; I am a wife,
a mother; if robbed by an incensed father of the
first title, the last would only double my misery.
In human life, the least must of necessity yield to
the greater duty. Reason, nature, law, choice,
make me yours for ever: nor can even the power
of a parent break the tie he voluntarily hallowed.
A mind so generous and dispassionate as Dr.

Dalton's, will surely see, that, in thus disappearing from society, I rather seek to guard from another bloody contention two fiery spirits, who severally claim so dear a right in me, that, to one or the other, I should be every moment in danger of falling a victim, than to indulge a bold and romantic passion." — " Emily," solemnly repeated the Marquis, " I am yours — for ever yours; the miseries which I have caused you to endure entitle you to judge for both of us. Greatly have *I* erred; may I alone err! Use the power I now so fully give you, more wisely than I have used mine."

Morning carried away the Marquis, no more to haunt the beloved shades of Frescati. Noon set down Emily at the house of the kind Physician; who welcomed her with the happy news, that her babe appeared to have escaped the infection. Mrs. Dalton took the mother to her bosom, with as kind a greeting as she had given the infant; and, conducting her to an elegant apartment, entreated her to be there entirely at home.

The first few hours were spent by all parties in those ingratiating attentions that insensibly remove the impression of novelty from a scene or acquaintance. Upon the approaching evening, Emily began to be painfully sensible of the difficult task which she had taken on herself, when she engaged to interest absolute strangers in her fate and her feelings, while she had unwarily deprived her heart of its dearest adviser, support and consolation. Overwhelmed with these agitating reflections, her tears flowed in silence; and Mrs. Dalton, moved by her extreme youth, and her deep mourning, found so natural a grief but too infectious.

Dr. Dalton, on rejoining the ladies, sought to divert the thoughts of both from sorrowful ideas, by interesting them in the account he gave of a young Englishman, who, without a regular introduction, had just applied to him for advice, and won him to regard. He expressed great impatience for the morning, when the stranger had promised him a more full knowledge of his situation, both in fortune and feelings; which his dignity of mien, and intelligent countenance, made matter of great curiosity. A vague kind of apprehension seized on Emily; who faintly inquired if the stranger was pale, and had been wounded?

Dr. Dalton assented; dwelling anew on his air
of distinction, and "that noble kind of physiog-
nomy which an enlightened mind alone can give
even to correct beauty." The flutter of Sir
Edward's daughter increased; and Dr. Dalton
wistfully surveyed her fair cheeks, on which,
in spite of the efforts of her reason, glowed
the tender alarms of her heart; while her ingenuous eyes, ever ready to convey its meaning,
escaped those of her observing friend only by
seeking the ground. " You are, perhaps, Madam,"
said the Doctor, after a pause, " already acquainted
with this interesting stranger?" Emily shook
her head, sighed, but trusted not her lips with a
syllable. He again paused; then continued his
discourse. " It is, I dare say, impossible to be
much with you, and think of any thing distinct
from yourself. I can no otherwise account for
the singular idea that haunts me, of a striking
resemblance between my unknown visitor and Sir
Edward Arden. Yet, the youth's complexion is
not so dark, and his hair a bright auburn : it is
the form of his face — something familiar to my
ear in the tone of his voice — but, above all, the
grace of his manner, that seemed to present the
very man to my mind."

Emily clasped her hands in silence at the imprudence of the Marquis, whom she recognised in every particular Dr. Dalton dwelt on, but remained determinately silent : and her tears might well be imputed to painful recollections that had no reference to the stranger.   He would have vanished from the mind of Dr. Dalton, had not a billet been brought, half an hour after, to Emily. — "Proceed and prosper, my beloved, I could not resist my racking desire to see this friend, on whom you have made me dependent ; and find in his countenance that prepossessing benignity which his voice confirms.   Act upon his generous feelings with your best speed, that you may become wholly his, who knows not how to live a day without you.   All my objections to your proposed deception vanished the moment I could no longer behold you.   Early in the morning, I will send for your answer : would we were, till then, with the Dryads at Frescati."

The surprise which Dr. Dalton and his lady felt at finding their lovely guest, whom they supposed to be without one friend or connection in Rome, was already greeted by a correspondent, increased greatly on perceiving Emily's agitation.   The moment her eye glanced on the superscription, hardly could her trembling fingers break the seal — her overflowing eyes connect the words — or her perturbed mind conceive their purport.   Yet her native ingenuousness told her that the smallest reserve, the least hesitation, might give her new friends the most humiliating impression of her conduct.   She therefore folded the billet, and, with a dignified tenderness kissing it first, put it into her bosom, and led to an immediate explanation of the mystery which it implied.

So touching, though simple, was her little history, that it hardly needed the graces which her drooping youth, exquisite beauty, and tearful sensibility, gave it to her hearers.   The forms of life were instantaneously swallowed up in its feelings. Dr. Dalton and his lady embarked at once in her situation, joyed in her joys, suffered in her sufferings; glowed with her indignation at the recital of Sir Edward's harshness, and shrunk finally with her horror when she told them that it had been his cruel hand which had struck at the life of her husband.   They vowed to renounce the father; while to the fair unfortunate daughter, they promised unalterable friendship, paternal affection.

At this crisis in Emily's narrative, the nurse happened to bring in the babe for the evening blessing of the tender mother: who intuitively knew how to heighten every generous sensibility she had excited, by taking her child into her own arms and dismissing the woman. This simple effect of a delicate tenderness awakened the most lively sympathy for the Marquis, of whose prolonged existence she well knew that she necessarily soon must speak. Enlightened by a word, as to the visitor of the evening, Dr. Dalton deeply regretted not knowing the truth before the Marquis withdrew. It was needless for Emily to plead the cause of her beloved : his pale and anxious countenance was yet present to the eyes of Dr. Dalton, and had already so prepossessed him, that the worthy man declared it would have been impossible for any human being, so painfully circumstanced, to have avoided his error; though few would have made so ample an atonement for it. Far, he added, from approving Sir Edward Arden's conduct, he applauded that of his daughter, and should receive the husband with the same cordiality he had the wife; nor would he hesitate to assist in any measure proposed for perpetuating the union

of a pair so formed for each other. The tears of
apprehension were yet undried on the cheeks of
Emily, when those of transport washed them away:
— her beauty assumed almost a celestial charm,
when lighted up by gratitude.

The warm heart of Dr. Dalton made him now
grieve that he knew not where to find the Marquis; for then would he have hastened to add him
to the little party: " so should no one heart in it
be ill at ease." — Alas! good man! had he been
twenty years younger, well would he have guessed
that he need not look far for a lover so anxious;
who past half the night in wandering near the
house that contained his treasure. It is possible
Emily could have quickened her friend's perception,
but that she had a task to execute, which admitted not an abrupt avowal that the Marquis yet
existed.

In the exhausted state of her spirits, it became a
great exertion to communicate to Connor the
secret history of the midnight musician at Frescati.
But the ungovernable joy it caused in her humble friend was almost more than Emily could support: yet was she obliged to make a further effort
over herself, that she might talk down to ration-

ality the delighted creature. Even at last Emily was reduced to keep her for that night in her own apartment, lest, in the intoxication of the moment, the important secret of the disguise of the Marquis should escape Connor, and circulate through a train of servants, who did not now know that he was in existence.

With all her sensibility thus afloat, it was impossible for Emily to find any repose. If a momentary slumber came over her, she seemed to hear the well-known strains of her nocturnal harmonist, and starting abruptly up, paused — listened — sighed at being undeceived, and wished herself again at Frescati.

Morning at length came, and with it the messenger for Emily's letter. — Her joyful summons bade the Marquis assume any name but his own, and be a welcome visitor to Dr. Dalton. — Mr. Irwin was in a moment announced ; and received by that gentleman as a friend long known, and newly recovered. The melting sensibility which so many concurring feelings and kindnesses must necessarily call forth in the refined and generous soul of the Marquis, made him, in the eyes of all

the party, the most charming and interesting of
human beings.

A very short time gave Emily so unlimited an
influence over the mind of Dr. Dalton, that, what—
ever her opinion might be on any subject, he had
a singular facility in persuading himself that it had
been first his own. — He therefore soon found it
meritorious to assist the Marquis to run away
with his own wife; that once effected, all parties
agreed that Sir Edward might then discover at
leisure how to reconcile himself to the re-union;
as well as how to annul the ceremony of the marriage in Sicily. Having thus far carried the point
of embarking the Doctor in her cause, Emily
chose a moment, when she was alone with him, to
expatiate upon the horrors that had almost pre-
cipitated her into a premature grave at Frescati;
and seeing the strong impression the description
made on the worthy man, she represented how probable it was that some dreadful catastrophe might
again attend the meeting of her father and husband. — By slow degrees she reached the meditated point; and spoke of her being supposed
dead as the only sure way of avoiding any such

alarming contingency. — Would Dr. Dalton, she added, but sanction the belief that she had taken the malady now raging among her servants at Frescati, it would be no disgrace to have it reported that even his skill could not prolong her life. On the fidelity of her woman she could depend ; and in Rome the interment of protestants was more than private — absolutely secret. — A corpse might be easily substituted ; and if Sir Edward chose to see it, in a disorder like the small-pox, a parent would vainly seek to identify a deceased child. As, however, it was Emily's fixed intention to leave not only her daughter, but all her fortune, and personal effects behind, Sir Edward was not likely to have a doubt that he had thus lost her. Escaping by this plan at once from his power, and the horrors that tormented her whenever she thought of his meeting her husband, they might, without incurring the disgrace of an elopement, steal unobserved away together, and, in some obscure but happy home, pass those years which Heaven might please yet to give her father, unless he should in the interim relent.

Dr. Dalton listened in mute astonishment at this well-arranged, extravagant plan. He saw, at once,

that it would involve his character, perhaps endanger his safety, were it ever to be known; yet observing that Emily's apprehensive heart quivered
on her lips, he loved her too affectionately utterly
to despise her project, or treat it with ridicule.
The utmost power he had over himself, when she
was concerned, was to point out the perpetual
danger to which she would be exposed by her
interesting loveliness, and the youth of the Marquis.   The confidence she however had in her
own prudence, and the full reliance she placed in
the honour of her husband, made her treat those
objections lightly.   The inconveniences, which, as
the Doctor hinted, he might bring upon himself,
Emily more fully considered and answered.—It
had been Sir Edward's intention, when he left
Frescati, she assured the Doctor, to set out for
England immediately on his return: and when he
found himself charged with the sole care of so
young a child, the journey, she imagined, would
rather be hastened than retarded.   Should, therefore, any unforeseen occurrence (though that appeared to her impossible) betray to Sir Edward
that she was yet in existence, it must be when he
was far from Rome and from Dr. Dalton: for

whose honour and safety she felt herself deeply concerned. Her warmth had an effect in her favour which she did not foresee: a strange apprehension that she thought him selfish, if not timid, crossed Dr. Dalton's mind: and to avoid incurring her contempt, he risked deserving that of her father. He therefore dropped, at once, all opposition to her plan. This doubtful success was more than Emily had dared to promise herself; and seeing the Marquis approach, she left the gentlemen together. The conversation had been so singular, that Dr. Dalton communicated it as news to the Marquis; but found himself obliged to reconsider the proposal more seriously, when he learned that the husband, whom Emily, with sweet feminine affection, almost implicitly obeyed, had not been able to remove from her mind this cherished project. The manly character of the Marquis, however, gave it another complexion. He could not agree with Dr. Dalton in seeing the fraud in so serious a light. It rather appeared to him a natural means of chastening the heart of a fond, though mistaken father, from the pride and prejudice that had already destroyed his own peace, as well as the happiness of the two persons most dear to him. Her husband could certainly claim Emily, in despite of her father, would she allow him to assert his right and influence ; but as the bare idea of a struggle between two persons almost equally dear, half killed her, he foresaw that the return of Sir Edward would, even against her choice, subject her to his will. The plan in question did not necessarily lead to ill consequences : quite the contrary ; since, in the grief of supposing his daughter for ever lost, Sir Edward would be obliged more candidly to review his own conduct towards her. Perhaps he might then take the infant, whom he now appeared utterly to disregard, to his heart; and cherishing all its native elevation, gradually expunge thence the only littleness it ever knew. A friend, as kind as Dr. Dalton, would find a generous pleasure in aiding the workings of an ingenuous nature ; and might easily guide the sorrowful heart of a mistaken but affectionate parent. On his own part, every influence, both of reason and tenderness, should be employed to bring back, to the wonted habits of filial affection and duty, the beloved creature who was willing, for her husband, to become an impoverished wanderer. A temporary alienation, thus managed, might re-unite the whole family in an affection, the more tender and lasting, as it would be free from human prejudice, and refined by human suffering. The character of Dr. Dalton would be, he added, as it ever ought, always in his own keeping: since it would pain alike the unfortunate young pair whom he obliged, were he to incur a censure, even from himself, to serve either. The Doctor would always, therefore, be at liberty not only to avow the deception, but his own motive for joining in it; which, perhaps, as nearly concerned the happiness of Sir Edward as that of his children.

Further to engage the Doctor's sympathy, the Marquis ventured to entrust him with the tender secret of his wife's present condition; and nothing hitherto urged was half so influential. The fragile form of Emily had, even in the care of Dr. Dalton, almost sunk into a premature grave; nor did he think it possible that she should, in the same perilous situation, survive, if terror of mind were again to accompany those sufferings from which no kindness could save her. The tender husband, on hearing this, applauded himself for having implicitly indulged a creature, whose fate might easily become precarious. Reasoning was, from that moment, with him, out of the question; and feeling alone determined the future. Emily having, in the interim, called in a powerful coadjutor in Mrs. Dalton, the league was too strong for the Doctor to resist; though still his conscience secretly revolted at consenting to sanction a fraud of any kind, or from any motive.

News arrived the next morning from Frescati, that one servant was dead, and several more had sickened, with the small-pox. All communication with that part of Sir Edward's family was therefore entirely prohibited, and the Marquis began secretly to make arrangements for the flight of Emily; who now thought it prudent to impart the whole of her views to her humble friend Connor: and well she knew how hard would be the task of reconciling her to them.

How to the gross of soul can delicate minds explain that acute sensibility which, when once awakened, binds heart to heart, by a power discriminating as reason, yet impulsive as sensation — or, when once wounded, throws each in a moment to the utmost limit of creation? — It knows not how to qualify — descends not to contention —

disdains to be soothed — given to dignify existence, even though it entails sadness on those who
have it — a good never valued, because never
understood, by those who have it not. No human eloquence could have persuaded Connor,
that a being born to ride in her own coach need
ever know misery; or a daughter, inheriting a
fortune independent of her father, might be reduced to shrink from a power which it was at
her option to acknowledge. How great then was
the poor woman's astonishment when told that
Emily, instead of maintaining her own independence against Sir Edward, was determined to
fly from him; and not only to fly, but to leave her
behind! " So, after all her services, all her love,
her dear young lady chose to live without her !"
In vain did Emily represent that she was obliged
to leave her child to her father; and how could
she trust so precious a treasure to any other
woman's care? All the power which a rational
affection can exercise over a weak one, Emily
often exhausted before she could influence Connor; who, though she had learnt to hate Sir
Edward Arden's lofty spirit, knew not how to
respect it: and continually urged her lady to

consider only herself and child. Wearied out at last by the tender importunity and nervous agitations of Emily, Connor reluctantly took solemn charge of the beloved infant: consenting to confirm the account of the mother's death to Sir Edward, and for her sake endure what she termed " all his humours."

The Marquis had never resided long enough in Rome to be generally known; yet he was too much distinguished by nature, as well as rank, to venture appearing during the day: and the humiliation of stealing to his friends and wife made him, when once Emily was fully resolved on her project, impatient for its execution. Dr. Dalton purchased a travelling carriage; and his lady secretly made every necessary preparation for the flight of the married lovers.

Emily now secluded herself in her own apartment. The alarm of her having taken the small-pox was circulated through the whole family. Her infant remained, therefore, shut up in a remote part of the mansion; and the domestics, save Mrs. Connor, were prohibited access to the chamber of the fair visitor. Dr. Dalton, and his lady, with that favourite humble friend, were all

who entered it: and the servants had too great a
horror of a malady, already so fatal at Frescati,
to be tempted to break through the strict in-
junction.

Convinced even when the Marquis, as well as
herself, had gathered together all the limited
wealth they could, so circumstanced, command,
they would be poorly provided for the uncertain
future, Emily carefully collected her jewels, and
other valuables, to secrete them among the few
common habiliments she chose to allow herself.
— The yet untarnished bridal vestments she, with
a sigh, saw packed to remain behind; that no
visible deficiency in her effects might awaken a
doubt of her death in the mind of her father. —
Within her jewel-case she enclosed a letter in her
own hand, signifying that all it once contained she
had herself appropriated; nor was any human
being to be charged with purloining aught. — This
done, she locked the empty casket, and affixed on
it her own seal, with a written address to her
daughter: whom she exhorted not to break that
seal till she should be eighteen. — There was something so melancholy in these indispensable arrangements, each of which produced a new lamentation

from Connor, that poor Emily felt ready to sink under the task which she had imposed upon herself. — Yet she had only to recollect her increasing size, and fancy she saw the indignant eye of her father flash upon her, to return with fresh vigour to her painful employments. Dr. Dalton considered her pale cheeks, and high irritation, with great alarm: and, dissatisfied as he was with her plan, often fairly wished her gone, lest she should die in reality.

On the appointed night all was ordered within the house to favour the departure of the lovers: and the Marquis, an hour before break of day, came in the chaise to the door. — At parting with her little one, Emily sunk half fainting in the arms of Connor: yet when her friends again proposed staying, her resolution instantaneously returned. — She saw in imagination the husband of her heart stretched lifeless at her feet; and the voice of Sir Edward again sounded fearfully in her ears. " Farewell, farewell then, a while, my infant blessing !" cried she, folding the unconscious smiler to her bosom: — " for thy father, for thy father only, would I for one hour abandon thee :— but it will be thy happy fate to soften the heart of mine: — when he looks in thy innocent face, he will not see aught of the wretch now hanging fondly over thee, but rather the likeness of the nephew once so dear, so inexpressibly dear to him : — to you he will strive to atone for his past severity to both of us ; nor will bitterness mingle in the love which you may bear each other." — Dr. Dalton saw nature too highly wrought in a creature so delicate, and gave a sign to the Marquis ; who rather bore than led her to the carriage, which conveyed them rapidly from the dearest ties both of nature and choice.

It was soon circulated through Rome that the daughter of Sir Edward Arden was dead of the small-pox : she had never been seen there, and of course this was the news only of a day. The ladies spoke the following one of her infant daughter, as the heiress of two great families ; and on the third both mother and child were forgotten.

Dr. Dalton, who had only consented to countenance, not promised to support, the fraud, thought it advisable to absent himself from home, that he might avoid all embarrassing enquiries ; and, therefore, with his lady, went on a tour among their friends. Hardly had they quitted Rome before Sir Edward Arden returned there; and having, when he set out for Naples, left his daughter in the charge of Dr. Dalton, selected his house as the most proper one at which to alight. A strange and painful sensation seized him at suddenly seeing a servant of Emily's, who vanished. — That he was in black did not surprise Sir Edward, as all the family yet wore it for the Marquis. He continued alone for a while, and then was formally apprised of the absence of his friends: the regret he was expressing he, however, no longer remembered, when he perceived Connor enter the room; who, throwing open a mantle of black crape, presented to him the fairest sleeping cherub that ever graced mortality. — It was the first moment Sir Edward could be said to fix his eyes upon the interesting offspring of an unhappy love. — How forcibly did nature assert her rights over him! — He eagerly snatched the miniature of his Emily, and looked wildly around for herself. — " Ay, prize that jewel," cried the incautious Connor: " it is the only one, Sir Edward, you can now call your own." — A horrible sense of unexpected calamity weighed down the father: he turned, disgusted, and afflicted, from the savage who had thus harshly announced the completion of his misfortunes; still fondly clasping his darling babe, his infant Emily — alas! now his only Emily.

Stunned and overwhelmed with so sudden a shock, Sir Edward was soon after found by his faithful valet, who aided his recovery; and having in the interim learnt the ingenious fabrication of the death of the Marchioness, imparted it to his master; adding that the family at Frescati were still far from recovered. — There was nothing in a recital and catastrophe so simple, to awaken suspicion, or lead to enquiry. — Sir Edward therefore relied on the tale, and wept: — in Emily the Marquis died to him a second time; and it was his hard fate to blend the horrors of the past with the misery of the present loss.

A packet from the Duke of Aberdeen, which had been lying for some weeks at Rome, was shortly afterwards delivered to Sir Edward. Hardly had he power to break the seal: for what could it contain likely now to interest his feelings. The whole universe had not for him a woe, like either of those he must for life bewail. The letter proved to be in answer to that which he had sent, recounting the outrage offered to Emily by the

Marquis; whose prior marriage, and supposed
suicide, formed its whole subject. The Duke of
Aberdeen, never rigid, but always coarse and
worldly, began his epistle with reprobating Sir
Edward's interference between the young people,
when once they were united : nor did he less censure his listening to an idle, and, as far he was
empowered to judge, unsupported assertion of a
worthless wanton, that the Marquis had married
her. Had his son, in reality, twenty such super-
numerary wives, it would not be possible for any of
their claims to interfere with those of a lady of
Miss Arden's consequence in life, regularly, and
with the approbation of the parents on both sides,
espoused to the Marquis of Lenox. As his law-
ful wife, he was impatient to greet her : and bade
her fully rely on his ever regarding her child, or
children, as entitled to all he could bestow. Nor
was this strange interference on the part of Sir
Edward, the Duke added, his only or his greatest
oversight. The frantic passion that had induced
him to dispossess his daughter of the name and
title of her husband was more likely to render the
legitimacy of her child disputable, than the improbable assertions of any of those light ladies

whom the Marquis might be weak enough for a
time to prefer to her.   In fine, he exhorted Sir
Edward immediately to restore Miss Arden to her
rank, as wife to the Marquis of Lenox ; and if
she was sufficiently recovered to undertake the
journey, to hasten with her to England; where
she and her daughter would be fully acknowledged,
and all their rights legally established.   The
Duke concluded with observing, that he could
have pardoned a fond girl of Emily's age for
quarrelling with her husband about giving away
her diamonds and carriages ; but for her father to
expatiate on the loss of such baubles was unworthy both of his experience and sex.   He desired she might be told, that as a more magnificent set of jewels was preparing he requested her
to forget those, which it would be an impropriety
for her now to appear in, were it possible to recover them.   As to the Marquis, he did not pre-
tend to judge of his past conduct ; but he supposed
he would, in the end, prove no worse than other
people's sons: and when he had run about the
world for a year or two, and spent all the money
he could get, he would return to Emily in his
penitentials ; who, if she was as sensible and gen-

tle as she appeared to be, might then live better with him than she ever yet had.

The letter dropped from the hands of Sir Edward! A new light broke upon the deep gloom of his soul, which seemed shot from heaven to make his sorrows supportable. " The Duke then thought his son alive! — Ah! why, if he was not so?" — Well he remembered the idea could never have been gathered from the letter of his, that this epistle answered. To avoid owning, or denying, a deed that for ever clung to his conscience, he had simply enclosed the testimonial of the Neapolitan monks, which even detailed the interment of the Marquis. Yet never did the father refer to that affecting record.

Oh! how did Sir Edward wish that the heart, so powerfully bounding in his bosom, could have borne him instantaneously to England! for to doubt was to die. — Again he perused the letter; again assured himself that no father would so have written who had not been convinced of his son's existence. Another pointed conclusion followed; the Marquis was admitted to be gaily wandering with some woman;—who could it be but Emily Fitzallen? Ought then the father of his wife to lament that she was in the grave? With a head crowded with conjectures, a heart overflowing with variety of passions, poor Sir Edward cast his eyes around, and felt himself alone in the world;—without one human being to counsel with, one friend to comfort him. Suddenly he recollected Cardinal Albertini; and, at the same moment, that the truth, whatever it was, must rest in his bosom: since, though monks might fabricate a tale to deceive other persons, they would not venture an imposition on one of their own body. Wild with impatience, Sir Edward demanded his carriage; ranged like a madman through the house and garden till it was ready, creating new fear and astonishment in Connor and the domestics; then rapidly threw himself into it, and bade the postillions drive to the villa where the Cardinal usually passed the summer. Hardly allowing a moment for the greeting of friendship, the agitated Sir Edward gave that prelate the letter of the Duke; and, as he slowly perused it, watched, in silent agony, its effect upon him. The Cardinal read, and re-read, remaining long thoughtful; till Sir Edward, worn out with expectation, snatched his hand, and

almost inarticulately cried, " Lives he or not ?"
The acuteness of misery was in his voice, the
horrors of frenzy in his eye. " I know not,"
gravely, though kindly, replied the Cardinal,
" whether I ought to own, that even when I, in
compliance with your nephew's wishes, sent you
the attested account of his death, the true record,
lodged in the College, informed me that he was
recovering." The start which Sir Edward Arden
gave, the glare of melancholy joy that shot over
his care-worn countenance, surprised and shocked
the pious prelate. — Spreading wide his hands,
and wildly surveying them — " they were not then
dipt in his vital blood ?" groaned the agitated
father : " this heart is not blackened with the
eternal consciousness of involuntary guilt ? this
brain, this bursting brain, may discharge, in tears,
some of its anguish ; and in those tears I may yet
find virtue, — consolation ! Now may I venture
to visit the grave of my Emily, nor fear even her
ashes will shrink, as she herself did, from the
murderer of her husband. I am now then only
miserable ; — for this mitigation of suffering, let
me, oh ! God ! bow to thee ! — only, only,
miserable !" — The alarm and astonishment with

which the Cardinal heard Sir Edward impute to himself the guilt of shortening his nephew's days gave way to that of thus learning that the unfortunate young Marchioness was already in her grave: for he doubted not but that grief had destroyed her. He severely reproached himself for having complied with the wishes of the wounded Marquis, conveyed through the monks, in ascertaining his death to his family: yet, as not one word, in either transmitted account, threw a shadow of guilt upon Sir Edward, it was impossible to foresee of how much consequence to his peace the disclosure of the truth would be. In all Sir Edward had at first imparted, the Cardinal had seen only an injured, aggrieved parent's feelings; he thence concluded, that time, and time alone, could allay the keen sorrows separately preying on the hearts of all parties: and he was impatiently watching for the moment of general conciliation. That moment, it was now obvious, would never arrive. Most bitterly did he censure himself for veiling the truth, even from benevolent motives.

In the uncontrollable restlessness of a wounded mind, Sir Edward was now equally eager to fly to Frescati; whither his venerable friend insisted on accompanying him. In the way thither, the latter first learned that the malady was yet among the servants, to which the young lady was concluded to have been a victim. It was some relief to the Cardinal, to find that a natural, and not a mental calamity, had thus early subjected Emily to the stroke of mortality.

What a state is his who feels a deep sense of unkindness to an object still exquisitely dear, though for ever vanished! The tear that would have melted the beloved heart, then drops like caustic on your own; the groan, which re-echoing affection would have impatiently replied to, then rings unanswered on your ear; and the deep solitude of the soul, amidst all the distracting tumults of an ever busy, ever fluctuating world, becomes an awful punishment, even before the final audit.

Sir Edward once more found himself upon the threshold of his villa at Frescati: still was the sad moment present to his mind, when he came thither to receive the lovely, unfortunate Emily, before yet she was conscious of the misery he had brought upon her youth. Again she threw herself into his paternal arms, as certain of pity, protection, fondness; his secret soul told him that she found not these poor alleviations of irremediable calamity. Again she seemed, in the agony of conjugal love, to spring from those arms, as though a single word had snapt the weaker chord of nature: and starting — he felt himself childless. — He vainly wept; vainly he smote his bosom; blending all the misery of a late repentance with the keen pangs of parental anguish.

The Cardinal took upon himself to interrogate the servants, who were visible sufferers by the malady, which was said to have deprived Emily of life; and from thence he gathered such particulars as he hoped would lighten the affliction of the father. They all agreed that their lady had recovered health and bloom before she left Frescati; and even her melancholy had considerably abated; that she removed only to guard her infant from infection, and not as fearing it herself. To this information, the Cardinal added his own just remark, that, by going to Dr. Dalton's, the Marchioness had taken the best chance for life; since, if skill or kindness could have prolonged hers, she would not have died beneath his roof.

" He talks to me, who never had a child,"
sighed poor Sir Edward to himself; — his only one
was gone, for ever gone; repentance, sympathy,
sorrow, no more could soften, soothe, conciliate
Emily. · The mansion of which he was once so
fond now appeared a dungeon to him. Her works,
her musical instruments, her drawings, yet scattered about in all the apartments, gave various
forms to the unceasing sentiment of sorrow. The
Cardinal, apprehensive that he would sink into
stupor, ventured the hazardous experiment of recalling his nephew to his mind, as one who must
yet more lament for Emily. — " Ah ! yes, he must
indeed lament her," sighed the father; " for he
has purchased, by a crime, the sad pre-eminence
in suffering." Well now could Sir Edward calculate the excess of that passion which stamped
with horror the hours of bridal felicity. His
generous heart awakening to sympathy recovered
its spring, and bade him again receive the solitary
sufferer to his affection; so might they lighten to
each other a loss, which no time could repair.
But how was he to trace this husband, more
miserable than himself ? how make him sensible
of his absolute forgiveness, his anxious sympathy,

his eternal regret? — One link of the many which once bound them together, alone remained — it was the little orphan Emily. Motherless before she had known the cherishing warmth of a parental embrace; surely the father could not forget the tie that bound the grandfather? — Yes, the Marquis would one day assert his right in the darling child; and thus most certainly would he be discovered. But so fearful was Sir Edward become of losing the babe, by the strong desire his nephew might have to make her wholly his own, that he hardly would trust her out of his sight. As Emily had predicted, her daughter soon gained that indulgence which her misjudging father had denied to herself.

In turning over his papers at Frescati, Sir Edward laid his hand on the will, which he had so wrung both his daughter's heart, and his own, to obtain. It was, at last, of no use, if the marriage was not contested; and only a new cause of eternal chagrin. In observance, however, of the rational advice of the Duke, the Lenox arms were again painted on the carriage of his granddaughter; and she was committed, as the heiress of both families, to the strict charge of Mrs.

x 2

Connor, to whom Sir Edward assigned a very liberal stipend, and sole authority over the establishment of Lady Emily Lenox. He was not without a secret hope that the Marquis was even then keeping a strict watch on his conduct; which thus, indirectly, was calculated to convince him that he would always find the afflicted father tenderly disposed to a union of sorrows and interests.

Cardinal Albertini insisted upon Sir Edward's residing with him, as Dr. Dalton was absent; for whose return the Baronet, indeed, waited, to inform himself of such particulars respecting Emily, as he deigned not to inquire of servants: after which, — if in the interim the Marquis did not appear, — it was his full intention to set out once more for Naples, there to seek the treasure which he had learned, by suffering, duly to value.

Long might Sir Edward have waited for Dr. Dalton, who had quitted Rome with a fixed determination never to revisit it while the father staid, for whom his regard · had entirely ceased. He answered to Sir Edward's letter by a cold condolence on his great *loss*, but entered no farther on the interesting subject; and spoke of his ⸜ own return as an indifferent matter, wholly uncer-

tain. Sir Edward, piqued and chagrined at such
an alteration of conduct in a man whom he esteemed, and who had conferred a great obligation
on him, remitted not proper attentions, but hastily removed Lady Emily and her suite to the pu-
rified mansion at Frescati; after which he eagerly
set out again for Naples.

Dr. Dalton now hastened home, and was not
long in visiting Frescati, where he learned, with a
deep shock and surprise, the rational conduct and
manly grief of Sir Edward Arden, together with
the just distinction he had given his infant grand-
daughter, and the boundless fondness he expressed
for her. Connor, engrossed by the importance
and honour of her new situation, which gave her
the full command of all her vanished lady's rights
in life, could not find as much leisure as formerly
to lament the premeditated delusion, that Dr.
Dalton every moment more heavily reproached
himself for having become a party in. From
whatever cause Sir Edward had again absented
himself, not to meet him was a relief to the worthy man, as he flattered himself daily with the arrival of letters from the dear fugitives, whose
home he should then know, and could urge them

to an immediate disclosure of their re-union, which, it was very obvious, would have no ill consequence to any party.

Day after day, week after week, however, elapsed, without bringing one line from either the Marquis or Emily. Vague fears and alarms often agitated their kind friends, who now made every inquiry on the road that could be ventured without naming the parties: but so many travellers had passed since the fugitives, that no account could be gathered of them. Dr. Dalton too well remembered Emily had packed up rich valuables with their common baggage; and the painful possibility that her anxiety might lead the postilions to suspect this, and thus expose them to fall into the hands of banditti, haunted him for ever. Yet it was probable that the lovers had, from motives not to be guessed, changed their route, nay, even taken shipping. Whenever the idea that they ungenerously meant to ensure his silence, by leaving him in eternal ignorance of their retreat, crossed his mind, he hastily rejected it, however horrible the fear that sprung up in its place.

And where then were these lovers, so anxiously

dwelt on by the few to whom they were known?
In a very public and humble spot, where they
were passed and repassed by a variety of travellers, without exciting in any one emotion of curiosity.   Such is commonly the case with persons
travelling in a leisurely manner, and unattended
by a suite of servants, who, in reality, attract attention much more than those upon whom they
wait.

The morning broke upon the Marquis and
Emily soon after they left Rome, and gave to
their glad eyes each other, now most truly wedded, since without any equal claim or feeling, to
clash with a mutual, a fond affection.   The hand
of my father can never more be lifted against the
life of my husband, thought Emily; and she
gladly compounded for all the drawbacks attending this certainty.   Never can my uncle again
tear my beloved from me, thought the Marquis,
and turned, with contempt, from all which he had
resigned for her sake.   Incapable of personal
fear, the secret one that Sir Edward was even
now seeking means to annul the marriage of his
daughter, had always poisoned the pleasure of
being forgiven and beloved by Emily to her hus-

band. In the idea she was dead (for he well
knew Sir Edward would soon learn that *he* was
not so) it was possible he might sacrifice his resentments to the good of a child whom his pursued indignation would render illegitimate. Thus
might a few years, either by the death or marriage of Miss Fitzallen, and the united forgiveness
of their parents, render his appearance, with Emily
in his hand, the wish of all parties. Occupied
with thoughts like these, and a calm sense of happiness, unknown to each till the hour of their
flight, the fugitives passed unobserved. Emily
had never changed her deep mourning; and the
Marquis, to avoid observation, assumed it. They
claimed no consequence, but spoke of themselves
as having attended a young lady in a consumption
to Naples, whence, having buried her, they were
now returning to their own country. Conscious
of the value of their baggage, and afraid of others
suspecting it, Emily affected severe economy in
her travelling expenses; and found it a sure way
of being disregarded.

Whether the spirits or constitution of Emily
had suffered more than either could bear, or heaven
frowned on her flight from her father, cannot be

determined : but, four days after she left Rome,
she was obliged, however unwillingly, to own to
the Marquis, that she was too ill to proceed. —
A few hours gave a conviction that it would not
then be her fate to give brother or sister to the
dear babe whom she had left behind. Too late
did her husband regret acceding to a plan, which
his opposition, if determinate, would certainly
have ended; nor knew he how to procure his
Emily advice, or the least domestic comfort. —
She bore her situation very patiently; and making
the best of it, declared herself in a few days able
to pursue her journey, the fatigue of which she
supported better than her lord expected. They
beguiled the time till they reached the foot of that
stupendous natural barrier, the Alps, which they
must necessarily pass in the way to Switzerland.
In the visionary world which lovers form for themselves, happiness and Switzerland have become
almost synonymous terms. — The Marquis, and
Emily, might well think them so. — Still was the
hour fresh in the memory of each, when they
romantically crossed each other near Lausanne.
— The days that followed were the brightest in
the lives of either. Though their hands had long

been united, and their beings blended, time had not yet taken any thing from the charms they then found in each other. — To Switzerland it had therefore been their choice to retire. They meant to quit the traveller's beaten track, and seek some sequestered scene, where all the agitations with which they had struggled so long might subside into the sweet transports of confiding love and mutual sensibility. Dreams as aërial and delusive as these were absolutely necessary to render endurable, to those highly born and delicately bred, the inconveniences of Italian inns; where even the most distinguished travellers vainly demand the necessary comforts, for which they are exorbitantly charged. — The Marquis and Emily, with all their natural and acquired graces, while affecting an inferior degree, found it impossible to inspire that deference in these sordid wretches, which they only pay to the courier that precedes, the horses that draw, and the servants that follow their guests.

The little inn had nothing to keep the lovers within doors, while nature invited them abroad in a manner not to be resisted. — Over a deep and woody glen in which the house was seated, im-

pended an enormous mountain; on whose aged
head hung tresses of snow, which threatened to
enter the hamlet, with every blast that blew : —
beyond, and around, far as the eye could reach,
his numerous and ancient brethren, of different
heights and hideous aspects, with grotesque yet
chilling beauty, while they compressed the nerves,
gave elevation to the mind. It was a solemn
heavenly solitude, where the children of fancy
must delight long to linger. — Emily wandered
through the wilds the whole day, and playfully
made the Marquis, touching his flute, give voice
to the echoes of the mountains. — Their vile
supper had been waiting till quite spoiled, yet exercise and pleasure gave it a relish. The chamber,
like many which they had been obliged to tolerate,
disgusted them both — it appeared close and
humid, if not noxious — they therefore hastened
in the morning to breakfast under an arbour in
the little garden, where the Marquis gently re-
monstrated with the host for giving them so unpleasant a room. — The explanation that ensued
too plainly proved that a young person had only
the day before been taken out of that chamber,
who had died in it of the small-pox. — A dread-

ful faintness seized Emily — excruciating head-
aches followed, with other symptoms, which convinced her that she had received the infection. —
To attempt, while this was a doubt, to cross the
Alps, would have been madness: yet to remain in
this miserable inn, appeared no less detestable
than hazardous.   It was a lone house: and every
traveller, either way, must stop there.   The increasing illness of Emily soon, however, rendered
it impossible for her to venture over the mountains.

In these contingencies men learn all the value
of that foresight and firmness, which even-handed
nature bestows on rational women, to compensate
for the personal courage they are not possessed of.
Emily soon obtained from her penitent landlady
the best accomodation her poor house afforded,
and calmly retired thither, as to her tomb, after
engaging the two daughters of the host to nurse
and attend upon her.

In the fond apprehensiveness of a mother, Emily
had, from the moment she became one, endeavour-
ed to inform herself how to treat every malady that
might affect the welfare of her babe; happily, therefore, she had some judgment in her own case.
She entreated the Marquis, if she should lose, as

it was too probable she might, the power of en-
forcing her directions, carefully to guard her from
all mistaken kindness; and that she might not
fall a victim to an ignorant nurse, or village prac-
titioner, she obliged him to commit to paper what
it would be vain to hope he could, thus circumstanced, remember; requesting him to abide by
the system which she thus prescribed, whatever
the consequence.

The Marquis on his knees vowed implicit con-
formity: and having received and recorded her
injunctions, prepared on his part to fulfil the sad
but tender duty of watching by her sick bed, who
had so often, and so unremittingly, watched over
his. In a few days the delicate skin of Emily was
covered by the eruption. Her beautiful eyes were
sealed up; and hardly dared her agonized husband
hope ever again to see them open. Delirium followed; and only the voice of the Marquis, which
still she knew, which still she heard, in whispers
as fond as those in the days of bridal felicity, could
have saved her from the grave: but never did she
speak that he was not impatient to answer—never
did she extend a feverish hand which his did not
fondly receive—never breathe a sigh, which his
tender heart did not fearfully echo!

Three weeks elapsed in this miserable manner before the wretched Lenox could promise himself the restoration of Emily; and, what a ravage had that short time made in her beauty!—The Emily whom his boyish heart worshipped, it was plain he never more would behold. Those fine features, that skin more " smooth than monumental alabaster," no more would charm his sight; but the pure, the elevated, the generous soul, to which in ripened manhood his own was inviolably plighted, still survived the wreck of human beauty. A piety and patience so exemplary marked the days of Emily's suffering, that never, never, was she more adored, than during her convalescence: the only pleasure she found in recovered vision was to gaze on him, more dear than ought on earth; and had not the appearance of her arms told her what that of her face must be, she might have thought its loveliness improved, so animated were the looks of her husband at seeing only recovered life in it.

During this severe trial to the Marquis, he had a thousand times lamented having quitted the roof of Dr. Dalton, on whose professional skill he had great reliance: but never once could he resolve to write to him. How could he be certain that the

ingenious tale of Emily's death, which had been
fabricated merely to veil her flight, would not be a
sad certainty before his letters could reach Rome?
—Nor would he afflict a faithful friend in telling
him that they were overtaken by a calamity when
out of his reach, which he could so materially have
lessened had they remained within it.

Emily, though very weak, was now able to leave
her chamber; nor could her husband any longer
conceal from her the cruel change made in her
features to all eyes but his own:—as the conviction shocked her very sensibly, she anxiously
sought to learn his real sentiments and feelings on
so trying an occasion. He frankly owned, that
had he not been the daily, hourly, witness of her
sufferings, he might have been struck with the
change; but when he expected every moment to
lose the gem, he heeded not the casket that contained it: and since he still had his Emily, he
should delight, through his whole life, to convince
her, that sense and self were weak ties, compared
with those which sorrow and sensibility had formed
between them.—A certain noble reliance Emily
ever had on the few whom she could love, made
her, when thus generously assured of her influ-

ence, disdain to mourn such perishing advantages
as mere feature and complexion ; and, by exerting
the charms of her mind, as well as the softness of
her temper, she daily made a large compensation
to the husband who adored her.

Before she ventured to attempt the severe passage of the Alps, Emily thought it right to try the
milder atmosphere of the valley; whenever, therefore, she could induce the Marquis to hunt or
course, for the benefit of his health, she would
lean on the arm of her young nurse Beatrice, and
creep to a shady seat where a streamlet fell near
the road-side; this was for many days the extent
of Emily's walk; and having, with great fatigue,
one fine morning reached it, she was resting, when
an equipage, magnificently appointed, drove by
towards the inn she had quitted. A loud laugh
told her that the company had been tempted by
the beauty of the spot to alight; nor could she
hope to escape their observation. To complete
her distress, she perceived Miss Fitzallen leaning
on the arm of Count Montalvo. Yet her astonishment surpassed her confusion, when she saw the
Count, after pointing his glass towards her, drop
it carelessly; while the lady, glancing her quick

eye from a face that she no longer knew, to a habit which only attracted her attention as being English, turned alike away, as having regarded an absolute stranger. Altered as Emily supposed herself, it had never occurred to her till this moment, that she should be wholly unknown to her acquaintance: yet the painful chill of this conviction was lost in the happy idea that followed it.

How did she rejoice, when the Marquis returned, at the singular good luck which had caused him to be absent. — Nay, their having been detained at this poor inn became a subject of congratulation, since otherwise this worthless pair, who were set out to make, as their servants had published, the tour of Switzerland, would infallibly have disturbed their repose before they could have breathed in their chosen asylum.

The Marquis with indignation exclaimed that he knew not, now, where to look for 'a peaceful retreat. — " Say not so, my love, for I can point out a safe and pleasant one," cried Emily : " let us avail ourselves of my misfortune, and, since my features are altered past recollection, let us at least escape for ever the woman who yet might find means to embitter our fate. — There is a spot

where we may learn from day to day, and year to
year, and that without a single inquiry, or one
confidant, all that interests our feelings : my cruel
malady, to my deeper thought, seems sent by
heaven to ascertain our peace. — No eye shall
henceforward know Sir Edward Arden's daughter,
save yours — no heart acknowledge her ; — those
native wilds which without you I detested, with
you I shall find paradise : nor will the long hated
Bellarney appear to you a cheerless residence. —
The mansion will doubtless be wholly deserted
during the infancy of our Emily, for my father
never since he lost my mother set foot within it
voluntarily. — At the bottom of the hill upon
which it is seated, a wild romantic river winds to
the sea ; — on its banks are many cabins beauti-
fully situated : some one will surely bear improving.
There, untitled and unknown, may we fix our
abode, and wait the course of time, apparently as
contented tenants to our own sweet daughter."

The glow of mind which the Marchioness ever
threw over her projects, the heart of her husband
had been used to catch : if they must bury themselves, no place was indeed so eligible. He well
knew Emily might indeed appear as a stranger,

even on her own domains; and he had never set
foot on the shore of Ireland. Bellarney had not
merely the advantage of being the spot where they
could, without difficulty, learn all they might want
to know, but the only one where they were sure
of never being sought for. Above all, it was the
residence Emily preferred; and to make her happy
was so entirely the wish of her husband, that he
would hardly, to his own heart, admit it to be a
duty. How, how could he ever merit or return
the sacrifices she had made for him? For him
she had quitted her father; nay, for him awhile
torn herself from her infant daughter! for him,
without a murmur, lost her beauty! for him resigned a splendid fortune, and a favourite home!
When he discovered how inherent the love of that
home was, well could he calculate the value she
set on those goods, of which this was the least:
well, too, could he estimate his own consequence
with her; since, in renouncing them, he was the
only equivalent she desired. Nor did she desire
in vain. The generous nature of the Marquis
rendered her, in a love that never swerved, a faith
till death unbroken, the return, the sole return,
which Emily would have accepted.

Whenever they were out of Italy, to write to
Dr. Dalton the Marquis thought would be absolutely indispensable; but on this point Emily did
not agree with him.   She found such a sense of
safety in having wholly escaped, and had so strong
an apprehension that to keep up, in a retired spot
in Ireland, any correspondence in Italy would
sooner or later betray them, that she persuaded
him to withhold the promised information, in the
belief that the reasons upon which they acted
would always make their peace with a true friend.
It, however, occurred to Emily, that the alteration
of her features might one day render it difficult to
identify herself, even on her own domains.   She,
therefore, thought it a prudent precaution to take
Beatrice with them as a witness, at any future
period, that it was at this very time and place, she
had been so changed by the cruel malady.   This
step would not lead to any discovery, as the young
Italian spoke no language but her own; nor could
know more of them than they were pleased to impart   Beatrice had attached herself greatly to
Emily ; and, as the prospect of seeing the world
is always pleasant at sixteen, she gladly consented

to abandon her parents, and her native mountains, with the travellers.

And now what became of poor Sir Edward Arden; when, on arriving at Naples, he found every thorn, yet rankling at his heart, sharpened, by learning, from the monks who had preserved his nephew, how generously and determinately that young man screened him from the odium of the duel, and how tenderly he had ever mentioned his uncle? Yet, by their account, the Marquis had been very unfit for a journey when he left Naples; nor was there a clue by which he might afterwards be traced. If, as was probable, the news of Emily's death had reached him while in a weak state of mind and body, it was but too likely that the heart-broken husband should, as the priests surmised, have entombed himself in La Trappe, or some other monastery. Again, therefore, was the disappointed heart of Sir Edward Arden without a resting-place: — after again visiting the scene of his guilty fury, — again sprinkling, with his tears, the sod where the beloved victim had fallen, he found no alternative but once more to return to Rome, and intreat Cardinal Albertini to use his influence in exploring the Carthusian, and other monasteries, where it might be likely his afflicted nephew had taken refuge.

On reaching Rome, a new shock awaited Sir Edward;—the worthy Dr. Dalton had expired suddenly of an apoplexy; and Mrs. Dalton had left that city for Montpelier, from whence the Doctor married her. At Frescati, the baronet, however, found his grand-daughter well, and daily improving in strength and beauty. Letters from the Duke, he learnt, had been long lying at Rome for him, which he now tore open with agonised impatience. He found in them only a condolence on the death of the Marchioness, and a very severe censure of her husband, as the supposed cause, by previous unkindness towards her. Again the Duke exhorted Sir Edward to lose no more time in seeking a young libertine whom they should both see too soon, whenever he appeared, unless there was a great change in his conduct; and, for his further satisfaction, enclosed the only letter he had received from the Marquis. It consisted of a few hasty lines, recommending his adored Emily, and her babe, should it survive the misery it was now sharing with its hapless mother, to the tender protection of his father. He further entreated him to reconcile the misjudging Sir Edward Arden to himself; and finally implored all three to pity, and forget for ever, the unfortunate Lenox. Alas! how did this billet, which apparently had but slightly affected the father's heart, make that of the uncle bleed! The date, no less than the uneven writing and incoherent diction, proved that it was dispatched while the young man was in the convent, still fluctuating between life and death : yet, though writhing under the wound, no mention was made of it in the whole letter.

From the arrival of this billet, till his banker notified to the Duke that his son had at Naples drawn for some thousands through the medium of the bank of Genoa, that nobleman added he had heard no more of him; nor did he suppose he should, till he wanted money again. The letter concluded with another exhortation to Sir Edward to bring the little Lady Emily without delay to England, and explain, at large, the obscure business of the prior marriage; that, by the sudden and decisive steps which they should jointly take, the rights of the heiress of Bellarney might descend, without disgrace or diminution, to her daughter.

But of heirships, bankers, and bills, Sir Edward thought not; — his bleeding heart demanded still his nephew: nor could he resolve to quit Italy while there was one monastery unexplored — one chance unstudied, by which he might be found. Cardinal Albertini exerted all his influence to relieve the mind of his friend; and priests were dispatched to inquire, in every possible direction, for the suffering and melancholy fugitive.

Connor, being now assured that the Marquis was known to be alive, found her vulgar mind overcharged with the important secret that Emily was with him; but she stood in too much awe of Sir Edward and Dr. Dalton to impart it to the first without the concurrence of the latter. While she hesitated what to do, the news of the sudden death of that valuable friend made her the sole depository of the interesting intelligence. Doubtful whether she might not for ever lose the love and confidence of her lady if she avowed the truth without her consent, and always apprehending the severity of Sir Edward, of whose sorrowful feelings she was no judge, Connor, after many struggles with her conscience, resolved to maintain her promised silence. Nor was it possible for her to announce in what part of the world the Marquis and Emily had sought refuge; or whether, indeed, they still inhabited it: for Dr. Dalton having often discussed with her his various and melancholy conjectures on their long silence, left a mind, so weak and superstitious, rather disposed to conclude the young lord and lady both murdered, than thus deliberately dumb.

The journey to England, by land, with so young a child, appeared in all respects hazardous to Sir Edward. He, therefore, resolved rather to endure the tediousness of a passage by sea; and having engaged a vessel at Leghorn, provided with suitable comforts and accommodations, he took a kind leave of the venerable Cardinal; and setting out for that port, embarked with the little Lady Emily for England.

The amiable young man whom Sir Edward had been so vainly seeking, was now travelling peacefully and pleasantly with the beloved of his heart for the port of Havre; from which, as one of mere business, they thought it most safe to pass the Channel. Having there procured a vessel to themselves, they landed in Sussex; and crossing England to Holyhead without stopping in any

large town, they were soon and safely set on shore
in Ireland. Here Emily breathed freely; and
indulging herself with only a few days of rest, she
set out with the Marquis through that wild and
beautiful country for the seat of her maternal
ancestors—her own Bellarney. It was the close
of a summer evening, when they arrived at the
well-known spot; doubly pleasant to its owner,
since gilt not only by the sun, but by the rich
beams of early remembrance. In dear luxurious
silence Emily paused upon its

"Deep'ning glooms, gay lawns, and airy summits;"

while her lord imbibed from her a sense of pleasure
which the active soul of man is not so exquisitively
alive to as the more passive, but not less enliv-
ened, nature of woman. That sex, destined in a
manner to become stationary in the world, is by
wise Heaven endued with such tastes as will
always, well considered, make pleasures of their
duties. It is theirs to reign at home — with varying elegance to improve the spot on which they
are to dwell, and by bountifully dispensing around
the blessings which they inherit or obtain, find as
perfect a delight as moving in the enlarged circle

of power or politics can give to the man with whom they are to share existence. Who has not known the vague, but boundless joy of re-treading the spot which recollection first marks in the mind? Those hours and places when the soul knew not sorrow, the happiest delight to look back upon, and the most miserable revisit with a suspension of suffering: the roses that then bloomed before our eyes, the tree that then lent us its shade, will have for fond fancy a charm which the richest scenery must ever want, when the heart sickens with oppressive knowledge, or the eyes are dimmed with continual weeping. This spot of our birth, this little country of the heart, so dear, so inexpressibly dear to universal remembrance, might well affect the tender soul of Emily; since, though to the vulgar sense impoverished, she had brought back to the demesne which she dared no longer appropriate — the single treasure she ever sighed for — the beloved Marquis of Lenox.

END OF VOL. I.

LONDON:
Printed by A. & R. Spottiswoode,
New-Street-Square.

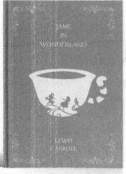